EASY REAL ESTATE INVESTING FOR BEGINNERS

9 STEPS TO BUILD PASSIVE INCOME, HOW TO AVOID COSTLY MISTAKES, AND UNDERSTAND PROPERTY VALUE, EVEN IF YOU HAVE NO MONEY!

CHAD K. SMITH, MBA

Library of Congress Control Number: 2025903600

ACKNOWLEDGMENTS

No book is ever written alone, and this one is no exception. I am deeply grateful for the incredible people who have supported, inspired, and encouraged me throughout this journey.

To my wife, Lisandra, and my children, Kendrick and Kennedy— you all are my greatest motivation. Your love, patience, and belief in me fuel everything I do. This journey would not be the same without you by my side.

To Randy Utz—your enthusiasm for life and real estate is contagious. Your ability to see opportunities where others see obstacles has been a true inspiration. Thank you for your insights, encouragement, and unwavering belief in those around you.

To Sherri Verdon—your dedication and expertise helped turn our vision into reality. Your tireless efforts, attention to detail, and passion for excellence transformed our dream home into a place filled with love, memories, and an exciting future.

To Noah Dodson—your integrity, heart, and relentless commitment to helping others are truly inspiring. Your kindness, work ethic, and passion for real estate have made a lasting impact, and I am honored to call you a friend.

To Shad Montague—you have been a mentor, guide, and trusted friend on my real estate journey for years. Your deep understanding of investments and market trends has been instrumental in shaping my approach, and I am beyond grateful for your support.

To Melanie Montague—your passion for real estate, financial education, and community empowerment is admirable. Your generosity and encouragement have played an essential role in making this book a reality.

This book would not have been possible without the wisdom, guidance, and encouragement of each of you. Thank you for being part of this journey and making a lasting impact—not just on this book but on my life.

With gratitude,
Chad K. Smith

CONTENTS

INTRODUCTION

Why You Need This Book

Every day, millions of people wake up, head to jobs they don't love, and feel trapped in a cycle of just making ends meet. If you're one of them, you're not alone. The good news? There's a way out. Real estate investing has been a proven path to financial freedom for centuries, offering stability, passive income, and long-term wealth. Unlike stocks or other investments, real estate provides tangible assets that generate income even while you sleep.

But getting started can feel overwhelming. How do you find the right properties? How do you finance them? What if you don't have money saved up? This book is here to answer those questions and more. Whether you're a complete beginner or someone looking to grow your portfolio, I'll guide you through the process step by step, turning what seems like a daunting challenge into an achievable goal.

Who This Book Is For

This book is for anyone who has ever dreamed of breaking free from financial stress and creating a stable, passive income stream. Whether you're:

- Someone who wants to invest in real estate but doesn't know where to start
- A young adult with student loan debt and no savings, wondering if property investing is even possible
- A first-time homebuyer who wants to make smart financial decisions
- An aspiring investor who fears making expensive mistakes
- A current property owner looking to maximize rental income and scale up

No matter your background, this book will provide the strategies and insights you need to **build wealth through real estate— even if you have no experience or a limited budget.**

Why This Book Is Unique

There's no shortage of real estate books, but many focus on complicated strategies or assume you already have significant money and experience. This book is different.

- **Beginner-Friendly Approach** – I simplify complex topics and provide a clear roadmap for getting started.
- **Actionable, Step-by-Step System** – Each chapter breaks down key real estate investing strategies in a way that's easy to understand and apply.

- **Creative Financing Options** – You'll learn how to start investing with little or no money through partnerships, seller financing, and house hacking.
- **Common Mistakes to Avoid** – Learn from real-life experiences so you don't make costly errors.
- **Practical, Real-World Advice** – I've personally used these strategies, and I'll show you how to apply them in your own journey.

How to Use This Book

This book is designed to take you from **absolute beginner to confident investor** by guiding you through **nine essential steps.** Here's what you'll learn:

- **Chapter 1**: Why real estate is the best investment for financial freedom, tax benefits, and long-term wealth.
- **Chapter 2**: How to find and evaluate properties, including off-market deals and foreclosure opportunities.
- **Chapter 3**: Creative financing strategies, from traditional loans to partnerships, crowdfunding, and house hacking.
- **Chapter 4:** How to negotiate and close deals like a pro, ensuring you get the best possible price
- **Chapter 5**: Property management essentials, including tenant screening, maintenance, and increasing property value.
- **Chapter 6**: How to maximize cash flow by setting the right rent, reducing vacancies, and cutting costs.
- **Chapter 7**: Risk management strategies to protect your investments, including insurance and legal structures.

- **Chapter 8**: Scaling your portfolio with proven strategies like the BRRRR method (Buy, Rehab, Rent, Refinance, Repeat).
- **Chapter 9**: Bringing everything together into a clear, repeatable system for long-term success.
- **Chapter 10**: Insights from experienced investors who share their real-world lessons and advice.

Each chapter provides **real-life examples, success stories, and actionable steps** you can start implementing immediately.

My Journey and Why I Wrote This Book

Let me introduce myself. I'm a retired United States Marine with a Master's in Business Management, and I've spent over 20 years helping people grow their finances. My journey into real estate wasn't always easy, but it transformed my life. It gave me true financial stability, the ability to retire on my own terms, and the opportunity to help others do the same.

I know what it's like to feel uncertain, to wonder if you're making the right financial choices. That's why I wrote this book—to be the guide I wish I had when I started. This book will give you the proper tools, confidence, and knowledge to **take control of your financial future through real estate investing.**

Real estate isn't just for the wealthy or the experienced—it's for those willing to take the first step, stay committed, and be a constant learner. If you're ready to start building passive income, securing your future, and stepping toward financial freedom, your journey begins right here, right now!

CHAPTER 1
LAYING THE FOUNDATION

"Ninety percent of all millionaires become so through owning real estate."

— ANDREW CARNEGIE

I want to start this chapter with the story of Sean Conlon. Conlon's journey to success began in the small, quiet town of Rathangan, Ireland, where he lived with his parents and five siblings in a modest home. During his childhood, the family faced significant financial hardship, culminating in the bank's attempt to repossess their home. This struggle to keep a roof over their heads planted a seed in Sean's mind: owning a home could offer the security his family lacked.

Determined to make this vision a reality, Conlon saved up $500 over time and set his sights on Chicago. In 1990, he arrived in the city and took a job as an assistant janitor. By day, he cleaned buildings; by night, he worked as a painter in apartments. It wasn't easy, but Conlon's persistence paid off. After several years of hard work, he had saved enough money in a shoebox to purchase his first apartment.

When Conlon sold his first apartment, he made $4,000—an amount that served as both a financial boost and a motivational spark. The success of his first sale pushed him to continue investing in real estate. Over time, Conlon's income increased to around $14,000 annually, prompting him to venture into selling real estate as a side job. For three years, he balanced his work as an investor and his real estate sales until he became one of the top brokers in the United States. He attributes his rapid success to an unrelenting work ethic and a determination to succeed.

By 1996, Conlon had achieved his first major financial milestone: he became a millionaire. His deep understanding of zoning laws and lot sizes in various neighborhoods allowed him to capitalize on the booming real estate market. His ability to identify lucrative investment properties further accelerated his wealth-building efforts. In 2000, Conlon took a significant step in his career by founding his own real estate investment firm, Conlon & Co. Through hard work, dedication, and a strategic understanding of the real estate market, Sean Conlon turned his modest beginnings into a thriving business, becoming a model of perseverance and success (Stevens 2024).

And this story isn't even a unique one. Hundreds of thousands of people have turned their lives around and found success through real estate investing. If they can do it, you can too.

In this chapter, we'll get straight to the point. You'll learn why real estate is one of the most reliable ways to build wealth and how it offers tangible benefits like capital growth and passive income. We'll focus on developing the right mindset—a no-nonsense, hard-driving mentality that pushes through challenges and sees opportunities where others see obstacles. And we'll show you how to set clear, actionable financial goals—goals that will keep you on track and moving forward.

Why Invest in Real Estate?

Before we get started, let's look at why people want to invest in real estate. When comparing real estate to other investment options, such as stocks and bonds, several unique features stand out. Real estate offers a level of stability and predictability that many find appealing. Unlike the stock market, which can experience wild fluctuations, real estate tends to move in more predictable cycles (Bankwest n.d.). This makes it a favorite among those seeking a steady investment. Another significant advantage is the tangibility and control real estate offers. Unlike stocks, which can feel abstract and distant, real estate is something you can see and touch. This tangible nature gives investors a sense of control that other investments may lack. You can make decisions about property improvements or management strategies, directly influencing your investment's performance. This hands-on approach appeals to those who prefer to actively engage with their investments rather than passively watch from the sidelines.

Investing in real estate is viewed as a way to build wealth and generate income over time. With the potential for both capital growth and steady rental income, real estate investments can provide both immediate and long-term financial benefits. As Franklin D. Roosevelt said, "Real estate cannot be lost or stolen, nor can it be carried away. Purchased with common sense, paid for in full, and managed with reasonable care, it is about the safest investment in the world (Goodreads 2024)."

Here's a more in-depth look at some of the key reasons to consider investing in property.

Investing for Capital Growth

One of the primary reasons many people invest in real estate is for capital growth, which refers to the increase in a property's value over time. This growth can significantly increase an investor's personal wealth. When the value of a property rises, it leads to higher equity, which is the difference between the current value of the property and the remaining mortgage balance.

Capital growth offers multiple opportunities for property owners. For example, as your equity increases, you can use it to fund further investments. You might choose to use the increased equity to buy additional properties, go on a vacation, or make renovations to your home. Alternatively, you may decide to sell the property once its value appreciates and pocket the profit or use the proceeds to pay down other debts, such as a mortgage on your family home.

Real estate investments also benefit from compound growth, where the value of the property increases at an accelerating rate over time. This happens because growth is applied to the increased value from the previous year. For example, consider a property purchased for $400,000 that appreciates by 6 percent per year. After the first year, its value would rise to $424,000, adding $24,000 to the investment. The second year would see a growth of $25,440, which is $1,440 more than the previous year, as the percentage growth is applied to the new, higher value of the property.

The longer you hold the property, the greater the compounding effect. Over 20 years, the same property would grow to $1,282,854 at the same annual growth rate of 6 percent. This demonstrates the power of long-term investment in real estate, where consistent appreciation over time can significantly increase wealth. Therefore, for those focused on capital growth, taking a long-term approach is often the most effective strategy (Bankwest n.d.).

Investing for Rental Income

Another major benefit of real estate investment is the potential for rental income. Rental income is the money received from leasing your property to tenants, and it can provide a steady cash flow, making it a valuable source of income. When the rental income is enough to cover the expenses of holding the property, such as mortgage payments, maintenance costs, and property management fees, the property is considered "positively geared." This means the income generated from the property exceeds the costs of ownership, leaving you with extra money each month. This surplus can be used for discretionary spending, paying bills, or reducing debt on your family home.

On the other hand, a property that doesn't generate enough rental income to cover its costs is considered "negatively geared." In this case, the investor must contribute their own funds to make up the difference between the income and the expenses. Although negatively geared properties can be beneficial in terms of tax deductions, they can put a strain on an investor's finances, particularly if interest rates rise or other unforeseen expenses arise.

To assess the strength of a rental property as an income-generating investment, it's useful to evaluate its rental yield. This figure helps determine how much income a property generates relative to its cost. Gross rental yield is calculated by dividing the annual rental income by the cost of the property and multiplying it by 100. For example, if a property costs $400,000 and generates $18,200 in rental income annually, the gross rental yield would be 4.55 percent.

However, net rental yield, which accounts for all expenses, provides a more accurate picture of the property's profitability. Expenses such as property management fees, insurance, vacancy periods, maintenance, and loan repayments all need to be subtracted from the annual rental income to calculate the net rental yield. Net yield offers a better idea of whether the property can realistically be held and whether it will produce a positive return after all costs are factored in (Bankwest n.d.).

Investing for Tax Benefits

Real estate investment can also offer significant tax advantages. One of the most notable tax benefits is depreciation, which allows property owners to deduct the wear and tear of the property from their taxable income. For new investment properties, depreciation claims can be made on both the building structure and items considered plant and equipment, such as hot-water systems, air-conditioning units, and even curtains. These deductions reduce the overall tax liability, providing a financial benefit.

If the property is negatively geared, the losses incurred from owning the property can also be claimed as a tax deduction. This means that if the rental income doesn't cover the expenses, the shortfall can reduce the amount of taxable income, which may lower the investor's tax bill. While these tax benefits can make real estate investing appealing, it is essential to keep in mind that tax laws vary by location, and it's important to consult with a tax advisor to fully understand the potential benefits and obligations (Bankwest n.d.).

In conclusion, real estate offers a unique blend of stability, control, and potential for wealth building. While challenges exist, they are manageable with the right strategies and mindset. Real estate's tangible nature, combined with its ability to generate passive income and appreciate over time, makes it a preferred choice for many investors. But how can you get started?

The Real Estate Mindset: Building Your Investor Confidence

Success begins with the way you think. Your mindset acts as the foundation for every decision you make and every action you take. A positive and determined mindset fuels progress, helping you tackle challenges head-on and find solutions when others see only obstacles. It shapes how you view opportunities and how you respond to setbacks. Having a mindset rooted in growth and resilience sets you up to achieve lasting results. This shift in perspective does not happen overnight, but with consistent effort, you can train yourself to think in ways that align with your goals. The power of mindset lies in its ability to influence your actions, your confidence, and, ultimately, your outcomes. Those who succeed understand the importance of building this mental framework as a basis for everything they pursue.

During my military service as a U.S. Marine, I learned firsthand how mindset could make or break any endeavor. Throughout my career, I pushed myself to excel physically, mentally, and emotionally. I earned a near-perfect physical fitness test score in boot camp (Parris Island, SC) and then finally achieved a flawless "300" during my time in Okinawa, Japan. Teaching the Marine Corps Martial Arts Program to Russians in Vladivostok further demonstrated how far determination and discipline could take you. My days were filled with rigorous activities like snorkeling, grappling, boxing, and running, each designed to sharpen my skills and test my limits. I thrived on the camaraderie and the constant drive to improve, and I found satisfaction in overcoming every challenge put before me.

However, life does not follow a predictable trajectory. My time in Iraq during Operation Enduring Freedom in 2003 and Operation Iraqi Freedom in 2004 brought unforeseen challenges. The physical and mental scars I carried from these experiences changed everything. In 2004, injuries left me facing a future I had not prepared for. Pain and dependence on nearly thirty prescriptions overshadowed the discipline and strength I had once taken for granted. At my lowest, I questioned whether I could rebuild my life. Despair became a daily struggle, and I felt as though everything I had achieved was slipping away.

A turning point came in the form of a conversation with Commander Borowvy. Her blunt but honest words shook me: "If you don't change your mindset, you will die." That statement sparked a shift in my thinking. With the support of medical professionals like Dr. Michael Mountain and treatments such as the DRX-9000, I began the slow process of recovery. It was not easy, and it took years of effort to regain my physical health and mental clarity. What kept me moving forward was the realization that setbacks were not the end of the story but opportunities to rebuild and come back stronger. The resilience I developed during this period became the foundation for everything I achieved afterward.

As I rebuilt my life, I sought inspiration from figures like Brian Tracy and Daniel Pink, whose ideas on goal-setting and personal development resonated deeply with me. My faith in Jesus Christ played a significant role as well, giving me strength and guiding my decisions. I adopted the concept of "failing forward," understanding that mistakes are an inevitable part of progress. By reframing failure as a learning opportunity, I found the motivation to keep setting goals and working toward them. Practices like meditation and moments of stillness helped me focus on what truly mattered, while my determination kept me moving forward. The mountains I climb today may look different from those of my past, but the principles remain the same: persistence, self-discipline, focus, and a belief in my own ability to overcome failure.

This is the first thing I want to explain to any aspiring real estate investor. If you want to succeed, then the right mindset is essential. But what does the ideal mindset look like for a real estate investor?

Here are seven values that make the foundation of a strong real estate mindset:

1. **You see mistakes as learning opportunities**. Many new investors face the fear of making mistakes, which can feel overwhelming. The thought of losing money or failing can create hesitation. However, mistakes should be viewed as a natural part of the learning process, aka "growth." Each misstep offers valuable lessons that help refine strategies and approaches. Instead of fearing errors, you recognize them as feedback that contributes to growth. In real estate, risks are part of the journey, and learning from challenges can ultimately lead to better decisions in the future.

2. **You MUST have a growth-oriented mindset.** Developing a growth-oriented mindset is essential for

anyone entering the world of real estate. It's common for new investors to feel intimidated by the complexity of the market. However, you understand that abilities and knowledge can be developed over time with consistent effort. Whether it's mastering the intricacies of market trends, negotiating deals, or evaluating properties, you know that each experience contributes to your skillset. A growth mindset keeps you focused on progress, not perfection, and motivates you to keep learning and improving, even when you don't have all the answers right away.

3. **You identify your motivation**. What is your "WHY"?! Understanding why you want to invest in real estate is necessary for staying on track. You must stay committed to your own personal "why". Many investors start with vague goals, such as "making money," but defining a deeper purpose helps maintain focus. Whether you want to achieve financial freedom, create generational wealth, or secure a stable future for your family, knowing your personal "why" can be a powerful motivator. It helps you make decisions that align with your long-term vision, commitment, and persistence to keep moving forward during tough times when challenges arise.

4. **You replace doubt with knowledge**. Doubt and uncertainty are common emotions in real estate investing, especially for beginners. The fear of making a poor decision or losing money can feel paralyzing. However, do you know that the best way to build confidence is through? Education. Constantly learning... studying market trends, understanding local property laws, and learning how to assess properties effectively can help you replace uncertainty with knowledge. Each

new piece of information empowers you to make more informed decisions. The more you educate yourself, the more prepared you feel to deal with the complexities of the market, making it easier to move forward with confidence.

5. **You start small but think big**. It's easy to get caught up in the excitement of real estate and feel pressure to start big. However, successful investors know that starting small is often the best approach. By beginning with manageable investments, you allow yourself to gain hands-on experience and learn the ropes without the risk of being overwhelmed. At the same time, you don't lose sight of your long-term goals. Thinking big means understanding that small steps will lead to significant success over time. As you gain experience, your portfolio expands, but the foundation you've built through smaller investments will be essential to your future growth.

6. **You focus on possibilities, not limitations**. The real estate market can be competitive and intimidating, especially when faced with challenges such as a tight budget or a saturated market. However, you train yourself to focus on the opportunities that exist within those challenges. A fixer-upper might seem daunting to others, but you see it as an opportunity to add value and create something greater. In a competitive market, where others may see limited chances, you recognize that demand signals potential. By shifting your mindset to view obstacles as opportunities, you open yourself to creative solutions and more possibilities, allowing you to approach real estate with optimism and resourcefulness.

7. **You commit to consistency**. In real estate, success rarely happens overnight. Many new investors expect quick results, but the reality is that real estate investing requires consistent effort, constantly learning, and the commitment to your purpose. Each small, consistent action compounds over time, leading to bigger opportunities and more confident decision-making. When you make steady progress each day, you will gradually see little chunks of success be rewarded as you stay committed to Your Purpose / Your Why, even when things don't move as quickly as expected. Never QUIT!

By building confidence through mindset, you lay the foundation for a successful investment journey.

Setting Clear Financial Goals and Investment Objectives

The right mindset is a great start, but it isn't always enough. Imagine trying to reach a destination without a map. It would be easy to get lost or take a wrong turn. In real estate investing, your goals are your map and your mindset is your compass, guiding you toward financial success. Setting clear financial goals provides the direction and motivation you need to stay focused and make informed decisions. Without them, it's easy to become overwhelmed by the day-to-day challenges or distracted by short-term gains that might not align with your larger aspirations.

One of the most effective frameworks for doing this is the SMART method. Originally popularized by management consultant George Doran, the SMART method is used across various disciplines to help individuals and teams reach their objectives in a measurable and organized way (Reed 2021). When applied to investing, it helps create goals that are clear, realistic, and actionable. SMART is an acronym that stands for Specific, Measurable, Achievable, Relevant, and Time Bound. Using this approach, you can turn vague financial aspirations into concrete, actionable goals that keep you on track throughout your investment journey.

The first step in setting a SMART investment goal is to make it specific. Without a clear goal, it's too easy to wander aimlessly, and chances are, you won't make meaningful progress. Being specific means defining exactly what you want to achieve and how. For example, simply saying, "I want to invest in real estate," is vague and offers no clear direction. However, "I want to buy a two-bedroom rental property worth $200,000 in a growing suburb by the end of the year" is a specific goal. Write it down! Specificity also involves understanding the purpose behind the goal. Are you investing for long-term capital growth, rental income, or to build a diversified portfolio? Defining the purpose behind each goal gives you a target to aim for. The more specific you are about your desired outcome, the clearer your strategy will be.

A measurable goal allows you to track progress. Without a way to measure how you're doing, you won't know if you're on the right path or if adjustments need to be made. In the world of investing, measurability provides benchmarks for success and helps ensure that your efforts align with your objectives. For instance, if your goal is to save for a property down payment, you could set a measurable target: "Save $25,000 for a down payment within 18 months." This is far more useful than simply saying, "Save for a down payment." You can measure your progress by tracking how much you've saved month by month and adjust your strategy accordingly if you're not meeting your targets. Whether you're targeting rental income, a specific return on investment, or saving for a future property purchase, ensuring that your goal has a measurable component allows you to evaluate your progress regularly.

Third, you need to make sure that your goals are achievable. The goal should be challenging but not impossible. Setting goals that are out of reach can lead to frustration, discouragement, and, ultimately, abandonment of your financial strategy. When determining if a goal is achievable, consider your current financial situation, your risk tolerance, and the available resources. For example, if your annual income is $60,000, setting a goal to buy a $5 million property next year without any strategy for increasing your income or savings would be unrealistic. Instead, a more achievable goal could be saving for a $100,000 down payment on a home or securing a 7 percent return on your real estate investments over the next five years. Achievability doesn't mean making goals easy. It means considering what is realistically possible with your current financial capacity and adjusting your expectations accordingly. Break down large goals into smaller, manageable tasks, and set timelines to achieve those steps, which helps avoid the feeling of being overwhelmed.

While "achievable" focuses on whether your goal can be accomplished, "relevant" ensures that it aligns with your broader financial objectives and current priorities. This step helps you evaluate whether the goal makes sense, given your overall financial landscape. A relevant goal must align with your long-term financial strategy. For instance, if you are currently focusing on paying off high-interest debt, buying a vacation home might not be a relevant goal in the short term. Similarly, if you're in the early stages of saving for retirement, investing heavily in high-risk ventures might not be the best move. Take a step back and ask yourself: Does this goal support my long-term financial well-being? Does it complement or interfere with my other financial goals? A relevant investment goal will integrate smoothly with your larger financial strategy and guarantee that you're working toward a cohesive plan that doesn't detract from other important priorities.

A time-bound goal has a clear deadline. Without a timeline, it's easy to delay or procrastinate, and your goal becomes something that might "happen someday" instead of a target you actively pursue. A time frame provides urgency and clarity, which are key for staying motivated and focused. For example, instead of saying, "I want to build a retirement fund," set a goal like, "I want to have $1 million in my retirement account by the time I'm sixty." This allows you to plan your monthly contributions, investment choices, and strategies to hit that target within a set period. Having a time-bound goal also makes it easier to assess your progress over time. If you fall behind on your timeline, you can adjust your strategies to get back on track. A deadline provides the necessary pressure to keep moving forward and ensures that you're continually advancing toward your objective.

Additionally, financial goals in real estate investing can be categorized into short-term, medium-term, and long-term objectives. Short-term goals often involve immediate actions, such as saving for a down payment or attending a real estate workshop to increase your knowledge. These goals provide quick wins, boosting your confidence and momentum. Medium-term goals might include acquiring your first rental property or achieving a specific cash flow target from your investments. They require more planning and effort but are crucial stepping stones toward larger ambitions. Long-term goals, such as building a diversified portfolio or reaching financial independence, paint the big picture. They remind you why you started this journey and what you hope to achieve. Prioritizing these goals ensures that each one contributes to your overall financial health and future security.

To help you set and track your goals, let's try a practical exercise. Get a blank piece of paper in front of you. Start by listing your long-term vision at the top. Underneath, write down two to three medium-term goals that align with this vision. Break these down further into short-term actions you can take within the next month or quarter. This exercise transforms abstract dreams into a tangible plan, making it easier to see the path forward. Here's an example:

Long-Term Vision

Achieve financial independence through real estate investing and retire comfortably by age 50.

Medium-Term Goals

1. Acquire five rental properties by age 40.
2. Build a real estate portfolio generating at least $5,000 in passive monthly income by age 45.
3. Pay off all debt by age 50.

Short-Term Actions

For Goal 1: Acquire 5 rental properties by age 40

- Research the top 3 real estate markets for investment within the next 3 months.
- Set aside $1,500 per month for property down payments starting next month.

- Secure financing and get pre-approved for a mortgage within the next 6 months.
- Purchase the first property within 12 months.

For Goal 2: Build a real estate portfolio generating at least $5,000 in passive monthly income by age 45

- Acquire 1 rental property per year starting with the first purchase.
- Increase rental income by 10 percent annually through market research and property upgrades.
- Reinvest rental income into new properties starting year 2.
- Explore multifamily properties as a way to scale income faster, starting in year 3.

For Goal 3: Pay off all debt by age 50.

- Begin aggressively paying down debt by allocating 30 percent of monthly income to debt reduction.
- Build an emergency fund equal to 6 months of living expenses within the next 12 months.

In this chapter, we covered the key elements of real estate investing. We discussed how investing in real estate can create financial security, build wealth, and provide passive income. We also highlighted the importance of having the right mindset—one that prioritizes discipline, patience, and long-term thinking. By setting SMART goals, you can stay focused and track your progress as you work toward financial independence. With these strategies in place, you're ready to move forward. In the next chapter, we'll focus on finding and evaluating properties. You'll learn how to identify profitable opportunities, analyze potential returns, and assess risks. This knowledge will equip you to make informed decisions and begin building your real estate portfolio with confidence.

Before diving into Chapter 2, I've put together two powerful checklists to kickstart your real estate journey! These simple, actionable steps will keep you on track and set you up for success so you can move forward with confidence and clarity. Let's make this happen!

Identify Your Why - Real Estate Investing Checklist

10 Action Steps to Buying Your First Investment Property

SCAN ME

CHAPTER 2
FINDING AND EVALUATING PROPERTIES

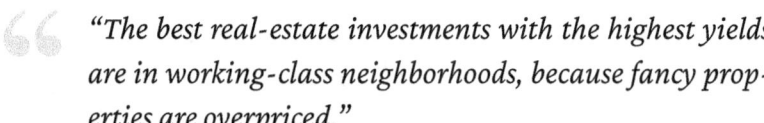 *"The best real-estate investments with the highest yields are in working-class neighborhoods, because fancy properties are overpriced."*

—JANE BRYANT QUINN

Now that you have the right mindset and financial goals, it's time to find and evaluate properties. But before we dive in, let me share a hard lesson from my experience...one that cost me more than just money and time.

It was 2004, and my wife and I were ready to buy our first home. This opportunity is a super exciting time in every person's life! This dream would be a place to call our own, build our future, and start growing our family. We had been renting for years and wanted to finally put our money toward something that belonged to us rather than throwing it away on rent. We found what we thought was the perfect opportunity—a 2-bedroom, 2-bathroom condo in a condominium complex called "Jade Coast." It was right next to MCAS Miramar in San Diego, California, and the location was unbeatable. The military base was just 1.5 miles away, so we figured renting it out in the future would be easy. It all made sense... until it didn't.

Fast forward to 2009, when the real estate market bubble popped, and our dream of homeownership became a financial nightmare. The condo we had poured our hopes into was now worth half what we originally paid. On top of that, we had taken out an interest-only loan—a decision we didn't fully understand then. Our mortgage payments had built up zero equity for four years— we were renting from the bank, and now we were drowning in an underwater mortgage.

With no way to recover, we were forced into a short sale. We were lucky to negotiate a deal where we only had to pay an additional $20,000 back to the lender, but it was a hard pill to swallow. The excitement of homeownership had quickly turned into a financial burden we never saw coming.

This is why evaluating a property beyond its location and initial appeal is critical. It's essential to do thorough research when buying property. Don't just look for a suitable location or believe that property values will always increase. Consider the long-term risks and the financing terms. Also, think about both sides of the market—the times when prices rise and fall. The right property can be a game-changer, but the wrong one can be costly.

So before you jump into real estate's financial waters, ensure you're fully prepared. Evaluating a property properly could mean the difference between building wealth and losing thousands. Let's make sure you're on the right side of that decision.

In this chapter we will walk through the following steps:

1. **Locate Potential Properties**. This is the first step, where you search for available properties through various methods, such as working with a real estate agent, browsing listings, attending auctions, or finding off-market deals.

2. **Conduct a Market Analysis**. After locating potential properties, the next step is to assess the overall market conditions in the area where the properties are located. This includes understanding supply and demand, average property values, rental rates, and economic factors that could influence the property's long-term value.

3. **Evaluate Properties**. This step involves a more specific evaluation of the individual properties you've located. During this stage, you assess factors such as the property's condition, location, local amenities, potential for appreciation, and the expected costs for repairs or renovations.

Locating Potential Properties

Finding the right investment property is essential to achieving long-term success in real estate. Whether you're a seasoned investor or a newcomer, understanding the various methods for locating profitable investment properties helps guide your efforts and maximize your potential returns. Below are several strategies for discovering properties that align with your investment goals.

Real Estate Agents

A local real estate agent can be an invaluable asset when searching for investment properties. Real estate agents possess extensive knowledge of the local market, which helps identify properties in desirable locations and gives insight into current market trends. Partnering with an agent provides you with a wealth of information about properties that may not be immediately apparent to an average buyer.

Real estate agents assist in narrowing down options based on your specific investment strategy, whether you're interested in flipping houses for a profit or acquiring rental properties that generate ongoing income. They can also provide you with timely updates on new listings that match your investment criteria. Agents often have access to foreclosures, bank-owned properties, and distressed homes, which offer opportunities to buy properties at a lower price. Working with an agent streamlines the process by presenting properties that already meet your needs.

Agents also offer expert guidance on pricing, negotiations, and the complexities of the buying process. Their experience helps them spot red flags or potential issues with properties that you might overlook, allowing you to make informed decisions (Steinberg 2024).

Multiple Listing Service (MLS)

The Multiple Listing Service (MLS) is a central database used by licensed real estate agents to list properties for sale. The MLS provides up-to-date and detailed information about homes on the market, including descriptions, photos, and price history.

However, the MLS is not accessible to the public, so you need to work with a real estate agent to gain access to it.

Once you establish a relationship with an agent, they can set up automated alerts to notify you of new properties that meet your investment criteria. This feature proves useful for investors who want to stay ahead of the competition and quickly take advantage of desirable listings before others. Since properties listed on the MLS generate significant interest, acting fast becomes very important.

Having a pre-approved mortgage in place is important when using the MLS because it positions you to act quickly when you find the right property. Additionally, understanding the local market and comparable property values helps you identify deals and avoid overpaying for an investment property (Steinberg 2024).

Online Auctions

Online real estate auctions offer an alternative, often less competitive, avenue for finding investment properties. These auctions feature a range of properties, including foreclosures, bank-owned homes, and distressed properties, often listed at lower prices. The bidding process can be highly competitive, so it's important to research each listing before participating.

One of the benefits of online auctions is accessibility. You can participate from anywhere, gaining access to properties across the country. Additionally, online auctions often provide listing details, photos, and other essential information, making it easier to assess whether a property aligns with your investment goals.

While bidding on properties at auction offers an excellent way to acquire discounted homes, it often requires quick decision-making and cash or financing lined up in advance. If funds are tied up in other investments, you may consider using delayed financing, which allows you to access cash from existing properties to finance your auction purchases (Steinberg 2024).

Off-Market Properties

Off-market properties refer to those that are not publicly listed for sale, meaning they won't appear on the MLS or other widely accessible platforms. These properties often present lucrative opportunities for investors due to the lower competition. However, finding off-market properties requires a more proactive approach.

Driving through neighborhoods of interest allows you to spot properties that might be in disrepair or show signs of neglect. Homes in need of significant repairs or renovations can often be acquired at a discount, presenting an opportunity for investors to add value through improvements. If you find a property that interests you, you can consider contacting the homeowner directly. Reaching out may allow you to negotiate a purchase without the need for an agent or facing extensive competition. Additionally, placing flyers or sending letters in the neighborhood to express your interest in buying can help identify opportunities not yet listed.

Networking also allows you to discover off-market properties. Sharing your investment goals with friends, family, and colleagues taps you into their networks for leads that may not otherwise be available. People in your circle may know of homeowners planning to sell or may have knowledge of properties on the verge of listing.

For Sale by Owner (FSBO) properties are another valuable source for finding off-market opportunities. These homes are sold directly by the owner, without the involvement of an agent. By cutting out the agent, FSBO sellers often save on fees, which might result in a lower purchase price for you (Steinberg 2024).

One investor, Dave Radelaide, found success with off-market properties by sending out a targeted letter drop. On his first attempt, he mailed 220 letters across 14 streets in two suburbs, carefully selecting homes using Google Maps and local knowledge to avoid recently renovated or unrealistic properties. This approach led to 4 email responses and 2 phone calls, which resulted in 2 offers—one of which nearly closed, but the seller changed their mind during the contract stage.

A few months later, Radelaide expanded his efforts and sent letters to 400 properties in adjacent, more affordable suburbs. While he was less selective this time, it still led to 2 interested sellers, and he ultimately purchased one property for $970,000. After investing $30,000 in updates, including garden work and renovations to outdated bathrooms, carpets, and lighting, the property was revalued at $1.05-1.125 million. The seller had been overwhelmed by the property's condition and was unable to make the necessary improvements.

Seeing success with this method, he decided to target properties that had been listed but then removed from the market without selling. With the help of a friend skilled in data scraping, he identified 10 properties in the $1.2-2 million range that had not sold in the past 2 years. He sent personalized letters referencing the features of each property he liked and explaining why he had not been able to buy earlier. This resulted in 7 responses and 3 serious offers. Radelaide ended up purchasing one property for $1.7 million and, 18 months later, sold it for $2.95 million, making a $600,000 profit after costs. This return far exceeded the market appreciation during that time (Property Chat 2023).

Preforeclosures and Foreclosures

Preforeclosure and foreclosure properties offer another way to find investment opportunities. Preforeclosures occur when the homeowner is at risk of losing the property due to missed mortgage payments but has not yet gone through foreclosure. Preforeclosure properties sometimes sell at a discount as homeowners are eager to avoid foreclosure. Websites like RealtyTrac and Foreclosure.com track these properties, providing listings and details about upcoming auctions (Steinberg 2024).

Foreclosures, on the other hand, happen when the bank has already repossessed a property due to missed payments. These properties are often sold at auctions or directly by banks, often at below-market prices. While purchasing foreclosed properties can be more complex and involve legal hurdles, it provides an opportunity to acquire properties at a lower cost.

Short sales occur when a homeowner sells their property for less than what they owe on the mortgage. Banks approve short sales when they believe foreclosure would result in a bigger financial loss. Short sales allow buyers to acquire properties below market value, but the process can be slow and involve additional paperwork. Keep in mind that short-sale properties are typically sold as-is, meaning repairs or improvements may be necessary before they can be profitable investments (Steinberg 2024).

Conducting a Market Analysis

The next step in finding a property is conducting a market analysis. A market analysis in real estate is a comprehensive evaluation of a specific property market to determine its potential for investment. It involves collecting and analyzing data on various factors, such as property values, recent sales, rental trends, demographic information, economic conditions, and local regulations. For investors, conducting a market analysis helps make informed decisions by highlighting whether an area is favorable for purchasing, flipping, or renting properties. It also serves as a basis for negotiating prices.

Here is a step-by-step guide to conducting a market analysis:

1. **Pick your target area.** You should begin by selecting a specific area where you plan to invest, such as a city, neighborhood, or region. Use platforms like Zillow, Redfin, or Realtor.com to explore the area's housing market.

2. **Analyze supply and demand.** You can determine the balance of supply and demand in your chosen area by checking how many properties are currently for sale and how quickly they are selling. Resources like the National Association of Realtors' local market reports or MLS data will provide insights. A seller's market with limited inventory and high demand might mean competitive prices, while a buyer's market offers more room for negotiation.

3. **Evaluate the location.** Research the amenities and features of the location, such as proximity to schools, hospitals, shopping centers, and public transportation.

You can use tools like GreatSchools.org to assess school quality and NeighborhoodScout for safety statistics. FEMA's Flood Map Service Center is also valuable for determining potential risks related to natural disasters.

4. **Assess the local economy.** Look into the economic conditions of your target area. You can find employment rates, major industries, and job growth statistics through the U.S. Bureau of Labor Statistics or local economic development offices. Areas with a growing economy tend to support higher property values and stronger rental demand.

5. **Examine local regulations and taxes.** You should familiarize yourself with local zoning laws, building codes, and landlord-tenant regulations that may affect your investment. Contact your county assessor's office to confirm property tax rates, which can vary significantly by location. A clear understanding of local rules will help you avoid legal and financial complications.

6. **Research comparable properties.** You should identify recently sold properties that are similar in size, condition, and location to the property you are considering. Focus on properties sold within the last six to twelve months to make sure they are relevant. If a property sells quickly, it may suggest that demand in that area is high. Properties that stay on the market for a prolonged period could indicate a slower market or that the listing is overpriced (Moore 2021).

Evaluating Property Value

When it comes to real estate, understanding the true value of a property is more than just knowing its market price. It involves diving into key metrics that reveal the investment potential and income-generating capabilities of a property. Property value refers to the estimated fair market value (FMV) of a real estate asset at a specific point in time. For instance, the property value of a commercial office building reflects its estimated price if sold on the open market.

How to Calculate Property Value in Real Estate

In real estate, property value represents the estimated price at which a property, such as an office space or commercial building, could be sold in the market. This estimate is based on the balance between market demand and supply as of the present moment.

- **Market Demand**: This refers to the level of interest shown by potential buyers or investors in acquiring real estate in a particular area.
- **Market Supply**: This represents the amount of available real estate (properties or land) for sale within the same market.

If the supply of properties remains steady but demand increases, property values are likely to rise. Conversely, if demand drops, property values may decrease. These fluctuations occur due to various external factors, such as changes in the interest rate environment, which affect borrowing costs (Wall Street Prep n.d.).

For a property value estimate to be reliable, it is important that the property has been marketed transparently. This means the seller must not conceal any material information that could affect the property's fair value. For example, undisclosed damages like leaking ceilings would influence the property's true worth. Furthermore, both parties involved in the transaction—the buyer and seller—must be aware of all pertinent details about the property and agree to the sale without any pressure.

What are the Commercial Real Estate Appraisal Methods?

Several appraisal methods can be used to determine the value of a property. These methods allow for a more accurate estimation of the market value, depending on the specific type of property and the available data.

- **Sales Comparison Approach**: This approach is often seen as one of the most straightforward methods for property valuation. It involves collecting data on recently sold comparable properties in the same area. This data can include details such as size, number of bedrooms, condition, and amenities, which are then used to estimate the price of the property in question. A benchmark value can be calculated using the average (mean) or the middle (median) of the comparable sales.
- **Income Approach – Direct Capitalization Method**: This method is commonly used in the commercial real estate market and focuses on estimating the value of a property based on its revenue-generating potential. To calculate the property's value, the net operating income is first determined and then divided by the capitalization rate. The result is the estimated value of the property.

This method shares similarities with the sales comparison approach, as both look at the market's revenue potential, though the focus here is on income.

- **Income Approach – Gross Rent Multiplier Method:** The gross rent multiplier method is another technique within the income approach that is used for a quicker valuation estimate. The gross rent multiplier is determined by dividing the sale price of the property by its annual gross rental income. To estimate the property value, the gross rent multiplier is multiplied by the annual gross rental income. While effective for initial assessments, this method lacks the detailed analysis of other approaches and is typically followed by a more thorough evaluation.

- **Cost Approach – Replacement Cost Method:** This method calculates the value of a property by estimating the cost to replace or rebuild it from scratch. This includes factors like land costs, labor, and construction expenses. While this method is less commonly used, it is particularly relevant when there is limited recent sales data or when the property is non-operational. It is useful in situations where other methods might not provide a comprehensive estimate.

- **Discounted Cash Flow Analysis:** A discounted cash flow analysis is typically used for more complex investments and projections. The process begins by forecasting future free cash flows to equity for the property and then discounting them back to the present using an appropriate discount rate. This approach reflects the risk-return profile of the property, with a higher discount rate indicating greater risk. Discounted cash flow analysis is generally more common in corporate valuations but can also be applied to real estate, particularly when evaluating long-term investments (Wall Street Prep n.d.).

Third-Party Appraisal

For larger real estate projects, especially in commercial real estate, it is often recommended to seek an independent third-party appraisal. A certified appraiser conducts a property inspection and evaluates it based on comparable properties, market conditions, and surrounding factors. Their role is to provide an unbiased estimate of the property's value, reducing the risk of overpricing or conflicts of interest that may arise from internal valuations.

Automated platforms, such as Zillow and Redfin, also provide property value estimates, but these are typically less reliable than professional appraisals. These platforms use algorithms to offer quick pricing estimates based on comparable property data, but their estimates should not replace a formal appraisal, as they may lack the depth and accuracy provided by a professional inspection.

For the income approach, the property value is calculated as follows:

Property Value (Capitalization Approach) = Net Operating Income (NOI) ÷ Cap Rate (percent)

Where:

- **Net Operating Income (NOI)**: The effective gross income (EGI) minus direct operating expenses.

- **Effective Gross Income (EGI)**: The potential gross income (PGI) minus vacancy and credit losses.
- **Cap Rate**: The capitalization rate, which is a percentage that reflects the expected return on investment for the property.

In this formula, the cap rate is determined based on market conditions and comparisons with similar properties. A higher cap rate suggests greater risk associated with the property, which usually results in a lower valuation (Wall Street Prep, n.d.).

Alternatively, the Gross Rent Multiplier (GRM) method is calculated as:

Property Value (GRM) = Annual Gross Rental Income × GRM

In this approach, operating expenses such as taxes, insurance, repairs, and utilities are not factored in. The GRM is determined through a comparison of similar properties, and while this method provides an initial estimate, it lacks the depth of the capitalization approach (Wall Street Prep n.d.).

Once you know the property's value, you can make a more informed decision about whether the price aligns with its market worth, income potential, and long-term investment returns.

Inspecting the Condition of the House

Buying a house is one of the largest investments you'll make in your lifetime, and making sure the property is in sound condition is essential to protect that investment. A thorough inspection can reveal both immediate and future repair needs, offering insight into whether the property is worth the price.

While skipping an inspection may appear to save money upfront, it could lead to costly repairs down the road. An inspection highlights potential maintenance or repair needs that could impact your financial stability. It also provides leverage for negotiating price reductions or asking the seller for credits to cover repairs. Skipping the inspection puts you at risk of overlooking significant safety concerns, such as mold, carbon monoxide, or radon, all of which can cause health problems. For "as-is" foreclosures or short-sale properties, an inspection is particularly important as these homes may present additional hazards or damage. Surveys from the U.S. and Canada reveal that the most common issues in homes are improper grading or drainage (35.8 percent), faulty electrical wiring (19.9 percent), and damaged roofs (8.5 percent) (Azdari 2023). Poor drainage can result in water seeping into basements and crawl spaces, leading to long-term damage.

Use the following checklist to assess key areas of the property and identify potential issues (Azdari 2023). Mark off each item as you go, and take note of any concerns that require further investigation.

	Description	Significance	Action Required if Issue Found	Notes
Structural Checks				
Foundations and Walls	Look for both hairline and larger cracks in the foundation. Horizontal cracks may indicate serious pressure and potential water leaks.	Ensures the structural integrity of the home.	Consult a structural engineer for assessment.	Pay close attention to any water pooling or soil shifting around the foundation, which may lead to significant issues.
Water Damage	Check for pooling water or soil shifting around the foundation.	Prevents structural damage from water intrusion.	Address drainage issues or consult a professional for repairs.	
Wall Material and Alignment	Examine the condition of wall materials (brick, wood, or siding) and check alignment using a level.	Identifies potential structural issues that may be overlooked.	Repair or realign walls if necessary.	Bowing or leaning walls can indicate foundational problems.
Electrical Systems				
Circuit Breakers	Confirm that circuit breakers are properly labelled and up to date.	Ensures electrical safety.	Consult an electrician for any issues.	
Outlets	Use an outlet tester to check the proper functionality of the outlets.	Ensures all outlets are functioning safely.	Repair or replace faulty outlets.	
Buzzing Sounds	Listen for buzzing sounds from the electrical panel, which can indicate loose wiring or connections.	Identifies potential fire hazards or electrical failures.	Have a licensed electrician inspect and repair.	

Plumbing			
Water Pressure	Turn on faucets to check water flow and pressure.	Ensures the plumbing system is functioning properly.	Check for blockages or leaks if pressure is low.	Low pressure could indicate a blockage or leak.
Leaks	Inspect under sinks and around appliances for leaks.	Prevents water damage and mold growth.	Repair leaks or replace damaged pipes.	
Insulation			
Material	Identify the type of insulation used and check its condition.	Helps maintain energy efficiency and comfort.	Replace damaged insulation as necessary.	
Moisture	Check for moisture in the insulation, which could indicate poor installation or water issues.	Prevents long-term damage and increases energy efficiency.	Address moisture issues and consider insulation upgrades.	
Roofing			
Shingles	Check for missing or damaged shingles that could lead to leaks.	Prevents water damage from roof leaks.	Repair or replace shingles as necessary.	
Gutters	Ensure gutters are clear of blockages and securely attached. Pay attention to flashing around chimneys or roof protrusions.	Prevents water damage and mold growth from improper drainage.	Clear gutters and check flashing for proper installation.	
Drainage			
Downspouts	Ensure downspouts direct water away from the home's foundation.	Prevents water pooling and foundation damage.	Install extensions or adjust downspouts as needed.	
Soil Grading	Ensure the ground slopes away from the foundation to allow proper drainage.	Prevents water pooling near the foundation.	Regrade soil around the foundation if necessary.	

Pest Control			
Termites	Look for signs of wood damage or mud tubes along walls.	Prevents damage from termite infestations.	Treat for termites and repair damaged wood.
Rodents	Inspect attics and basements for droppings or chew marks.	Identifies rodent problems that could harm the home.	Contact pest control for removal and repairs.
Potential Renovations			
Age of Systems	Consider the age of plumbing, electrical, and HVAC systems, as these may need upgrading soon.	Helps forecast future repair or replacement costs.	Budget for future upgrades or replacements.
Wear and Tear	Evaluate general wear and tear, including flooring, walls, and appliances.	Predicts upcoming repair or maintenance costs.	Address wear and tear with repairs or upgrades.

In this chapter, we covered how to find suitable properties, analyze the market, assess property value, and inspect a house's condition. We discussed techniques for identifying properties that meet your needs and how to understand market trends that influence pricing and demand. We also examined how to evaluate a property's value by considering factors like location, features, and condition. Finally, we explored how to conduct a thorough inspection to identify any potential problems that could impact the value or safety of the home. In the next chapter, we will explore different ways you can finance your investment.

CHAPTER 3

FINANCING YOUR FIRST INVESTMENT

"Real estate cannot be lost or stolen, nor can it be carried away. Purchased with common sense, paid for in full, and managed with reasonable care, it is about the safest investment in the world."

— FRANKLIN D. ROOSEVELT

Now that you've learned how to find the best property for your, the next step is securing the funds to make your investment a reality. In this chapter, we will explore various financing options available to real estate investors, breaking down their advantages and potential pitfalls. Understanding these options will help you make informed decisions that align with your financial goals and long-term strategy. This guide will provide a clear, practical roadmap to funding your real estate ventures, from conventional bank loans to alternative methods like seller financing and crowdfunding.

The importance of responsible financing cannot be overstated. In 2005, Casey Serin, a 24-year-old web designer, set out on an ambitious real estate journey, purchasing eight single-family homes across multiple states in just eight months. Relying on stated income loans—mortgages that required no proof of income —he exaggerated his earnings to secure owner-occupied loans with favorable terms despite not living in the properties. He also took cash back at closing on six properties, sometimes exceeding legal limits. When the housing market crashed, Serin found himself drowning in debt. Unable to manage the mortgages or sell the properties, his investments quickly spiraled into a financial disaster, leaving him with $2.2 million in debt and a negative net worth of approximately $600,000.

This cautionary story highlights why thorough due diligence and responsible financial planning are essential when financing an investment property. You must understand the loan terms, assess your financial situation by being real with yourself, and making a promise to your future about always maintaining manageable debt levels for long-term success. While real estate is one of the most powerful wealth-building tools, it can also lead to financial ruin if approached recklessly. Mistakes are part of the journey, but every lesson creates a smarter investor within you. To build this strong foundation, your self-discipline by constantly learning and continually striving for self-improvement will propel you closer to that financial freedom.

Conventional Bank Loans

Conventional bank loans remain a popular choice for financing real estate investments. These loans conform to guidelines established by Fannie Mae and Freddie Mac and are not backed by the federal government. They typically require a down payment of 20 percent, although investment properties may necessitate a higher down payment of around 30 percent. Lenders assess credit scores, income, assets, and debt-to-income ratios to determine eligibility and interest rates (Lake 2024).

Conventional loans can take several forms, including fixed-rate mortgages, adjustable-rate mortgages (ARMs), and jumbo loans. Fixed-rate mortgages offer stable interest rates and consistent monthly payments, making them suitable for long-term planning. ARMs start with lower rates that adjust periodically, which may appeal to investors expecting future income growth. Jumbo loans cater to high-value properties, although they involve stricter credit requirements and higher interest rates.

Securing a traditional loan involves several steps. You start by gathering the necessary documentation. This includes proof of income, tax returns, and details of any existing debts. Lenders will scrutinize your financial history, so having everything organized will streamline the process. You can work with mortgage brokers or lenders to explore your options. They can provide valuable insights into the types of loans available and help you navigate the application process. Understanding loan terms is crucial. Pay attention to the interest rate, loan length, and any fees involved. This knowledge will empower you to make informed decisions and negotiate better terms. Remember, every percentage point saved on interest translates to significant savings over time. As you move forward, maintaining communication with your lender is essential. Keep them updated on any changes to your financial situation and respond promptly to requests for additional information.

Advantages: Conventional loans often provide lower interest rates and longer repayment terms, which can result in manageable monthly payments and improved cash flow.

Disadvantages: These loans have stringent qualification criteria, including high credit score requirements and detailed documentation. Additionally, the underwriting process can be lengthy, potentially delaying property acquisitions.

Hard Money Loans

Hard money loans are short-term financing options provided by private lenders. They are ideal for projects like house flipping, where speed and flexibility are needed. Unlike conventional loans, hard money loans focus on the property's after-repair value (ARV) rather than the borrower's financial history.

These loans typically come with higher interest rates—often ranging from 10 percent to 18 percent—and shorter repayment terms, usually twelve months or less (Lake 2024). While they can be secured quickly, they also involve higher origination fees and closing costs.

Advantages: Hard money loans offer rapid access to capital and flexible approval processes. They are especially useful for investors with limited credit history or those pursuing time-sensitive opportunities.

Disadvantages: The high cost of borrowing, combined with short repayment periods, can strain financial resources if the property does not generate expected returns promptly.

Private Money Loans

Private money loans involve borrowing from individuals rather than institutions. Friends, family members, or local real estate investors often serve as lenders. Loan terms are negotiated between the parties and can range from favorable to predatory, depending on the relationship and terms agreed upon.

Private loans often rely on legal contracts, allowing lenders to foreclose on the property if payments are not met. While this option provides flexibility, it can carry significant personal and financial risks (Lake 2024).

Advantages: Private loans have less stringent approval requirements and faster processing times, making them accessible to those who may not qualify for conventional loans.

Disadvantages: Higher interest rates and fees often accompany private loans. Borrowing from personal connections can also complicate relationships, especially if the investment does not perform as expected.

Home Equity Loans and HELOCs

Leveraging home equity through a home equity loan, home equity line of credit (HELOC), or cash-out refinance provides another avenue for financing real estate investments. Home equity loans offer fixed interest rates and lump-sum disbursements, while HELOCs function as revolving credit lines with variable rates.

Investors can typically borrow up to 80 percent of their home's equity. This is the value of a property minus the amount owed on a mortgage. If a home is worth $400,000 and the mortgage is

$220,000, the equity is $180,000. These funds can cover down payments, renovation costs, or even full property purchases. However, using home equity involves significant risks, as failure to repay can result in the loss of the primary residence (Smith 2023).

Advantages: This option provides access to substantial funds at relatively low interest rates, especially compared to hard money loans.

Disadvantages: The primary downside is the risk to your home. Variable rates on HELOCs can also complicate budgeting. You also need a home to begin with, so it won't be suitable for a first-time buyer.

Commercial Loans

Commercial loans cater to properties intended for business purposes, such as office buildings, retail spaces, or apartment complexes. Unlike residential loans, these loans often involve shorter terms (five to twenty years) and may require a balloon payment at the end (Lake 2024).

Approval for commercial loans depends on factors such as the borrower's creditworthiness, the property's income potential, and detailed business plans. While they offer higher borrowing limits, they also demand extensive documentation and larger down payments.

Advantages: Commercial loans allow investors to finance larger projects with competitive interest rates and structured repayment terms.

Disadvantages: The rigorous approval process and high upfront costs can make this option less accessible for some investors.

Seller Financing

Seller financing, often referred to as owner financing, presents an intriguing alternative to traditional bank loans. In this arrangement, the seller acts as the lender, allowing you to make payments directly to them over time. It is particularly useful when traditional financing is unavailable or when the property has unique characteristics that make conventional loans challenging. This option suits those who may find conventional lending channels inaccessible, allowing you to step into property ownership with less initial capital (Lake 2024).

Advantages: Seller financing often features flexible terms and faster closing processes.

Disadvantages: Buyers may face higher interest rates, balloon payments, or limited property options.

Lease-to-Own Agreements

Lease options, or lease-to-own agreements, provide another pathway. Here, you lease a property with the option to purchase it later at a predetermined price. This setup is particularly advantageous if you're still building credit or saving for a down payment. It locks in the purchase price, shielding you from potential market price increases. Yet, it's important to be mindful of the possible drawbacks. If you decide not to purchase, you might forfeit any premium payments made, and there is always the risk that the property value might not appreciate as expected. Like seller financing, this method offers flexibility but requires careful nego-tiation to ensure it aligns with your long-term goals (Lake 2024).

Advantages: These agreements provide an opportunity to build equity while renting and require lower upfront costs than tradi-tional purchases.

Disadvantages: Higher-than-market rents and non-refundable option fees can increase costs if the purchase does not proceed as planned.

Crowdfunding

Real estate crowdfunding platforms provide a modern and increasingly popular method for investing in real estate. These platforms connect individual investors with developers seeking funding for property purchases or development projects. Through pooling resources, investors can participate in larger deals that would typically be out of reach, gaining access to diverse invest-ment opportunities (Hill 2024).

One major appeal of crowdfunding lies in its accessibility. With rela-tively low minimum investment requirements, individuals can start building a real estate portfolio without needing significant upfront capital. Many platforms focus on offering passive income opportu-nities, where investors receive dividends or profits generated by the properties without actively managing them. Additionally, crowd-funding enables portfolio diversification by allowing investments in multiple projects across different regions or property types.

Despite these advantages, crowdfunding carries certain risks. Investors have limited control over the property or project, as decisions are primarily made by the platform or developers. Platform fees can also eat into returns, potentially reducing overall profitability. Furthermore, the risk of fraud is a genuine concern; choosing reputable platforms with strong track records is essential for mitigating this risk. Some platforms also lack the regulatory oversight found in traditional investment avenues, adding another layer of uncertainty.

Advantages: Crowdfunding offers accessibility, lower capital requirements, and the potential for passive income, making it an attractive option for new and experienced investors alike.

Disadvantages: Limited control over investments, potential platform fees, and risks related to fraud or platform reliability should be carefully evaluated before committing funds.

Syndication

Syndication represents another form of collaborative real estate investment. It involves pooling funds from multiple investors to purchase, manage, and profit from real estate projects. In a typical syndication arrangement, a sponsor or syndicator takes on the responsibility of identifying investment opportunities, managing the properties, and distributing returns to investors.

The structure of syndication provides access to large-scale investment opportunities that may otherwise be unattainable for individual investors. By leveraging the expertise of the syndicator, participants benefit from professional property management, reducing the effort and time required on their part. Additionally, syndication often focuses on high-value commercial or residential properties with significant income potential, further enhancing its appeal.

However, syndication also has its limitations. Investors have minimal decision-making power, relying heavily on the sponsor's expertise and integrity. A poorly managed project or unethical sponsor can lead to subpar returns or even losses. Legal agreements and fees associated with syndication should also be carefully reviewed, as they can affect profitability (Lake 2024).

Advantages: Syndication allows participation in large-scale projects, providing professional management and shared risk.

Disadvantages: Limited decision-making authority and dependence on the syndicator's expertise present challenges for some investors.

Government-Backed Loans

Programs such as FHA, VA, and USDA loans provide financing options designed to support specific groups of borrowers. FHA loans target first-time homebuyers with lenient credit requirements and low down payment options, often as low as 3.5 percent. VA loans cater to eligible veterans and active-duty service members, offering zero down payment options and competitive interest rates. USDA loans focus on rural development, providing low-interest loans for properties in designated rural areas.

While primarily intended for owner-occupied properties, these programs can support real estate investments in multi-unit properties, provided the borrower resides in one unit. This arrangement allows investors to generate rental income while benefiting from favorable loan terms.

The limitations of government-backed loans include restrictions on property types and additional fees such as mortgage insurance premiums for FHA loans. These factors can reduce the appeal for investors focused on maximizing profitability (Lake 2024).

Advantages: Government-backed loans are more accessible to individuals with lower credit scores or limited savings, offering an entry point into real estate investment.

Disadvantages: Restrictions on eligible properties and additional costs may limit their utility for some investment strategies.

Partnerships and Joint Ventures

Forming partnerships or joint ventures allows investors to combine resources, share risks, and leverage complementary skills. These arrangements are particularly beneficial for large-scale projects that require significant capital and expertise. Partnerships come in various forms, such as equity partnerships and joint ventures, each offering unique dynamics and benefits. In equity partnerships, two or more parties contribute capital and share profits, while joint ventures are more project-specific, bringing together resources for a particular deal (Lake 2024).

The advantages of partnerships are numerous. Access to larger capital pools is one of the most significant benefits. Instead of relying solely on your funds, you can leverage the financial strength of others, allowing you to pursue more substantial investments. Additionally, partnerships bring diversification of skills and expertise. Each partner brings a unique perspective, knowledge, and set of skills to the table, enhancing decision-making and problem-solving capabilities.

However, it's important to be aware of potential challenges. Partnerships can sometimes lead to conflicts and disagreements, especially if roles and expectations aren't clearly defined. A solid partnership agreement will outline each party's contributions, responsibilities, and how profits and losses will be shared.

Advantages: Partnerships can provide access to funding, knowledge, and shared responsibilities.

Disadvantages: Potential conflicts and complex legal agreements can complicate these arrangements.

House Hacking: Living and Investing Simultaneously

House hacking involves leveraging your home to generate income, often by renting out part of your property (Araj 2024). The classic form of house hacking typically involves purchasing a multifamily property, living in one unit, and renting out the others. This arrangement allows tenants' rent payments to cover the property owner's mortgage, enabling them to build equity while minimizing living expenses.

House hacking offers a practical introduction to property management and landlord responsibilities. By living on-site, homeowners gain firsthand experience in handling maintenance, tenant relations, and finances, all while potentially having their housing costs offset by rental income.

House hacking can significantly reduce your living expenses or even eliminate them altogether. This strategy allows you to redirect savings toward other goals, such as increasing your emergency fund, investing in additional properties, or pursuing financial independence. For example, if you purchase a $400,000 duplex with 20 percent down at a 6.5 percent interest rate, your monthly mortgage payment might be $2,023. If a tenant pays $2,500 in rent, their payments cover your mortgage and leave $477 for insurance, taxes, or repairs. Over five years, with regular payments and home appreciation, you can build significant equity and even sell for a profit (Araj 2024).

Beyond the immediate financial benefits, house hacking helps homeowners build equity in their property over time, offering long-term financial stability and the potential for future wealth.

For those interested in real estate investing, house hacking serves as an excellent entry point. It allows you to learn the basics of managing tenants, maintaining properties, and navigating local rental regulations in a relatively low-risk environment.

There are multiple strategies for house hacking:

- **Multifamily Homes**: Purchase a duplex, triplex, or fourplex. Live in one unit while renting out the others. This setup offers privacy while generating income from your tenants.
- **Short-Term Rentals**: Use platforms like Airbnb to rent out spare rooms or guest spaces on a short-term basis. Research local laws and HOA regulations, as some areas restrict short-term rentals.
- **Long-Term Roommates**: Rent out a room in your home to a housemate. While this may sacrifice some privacy, it can significantly lower your housing costs. Establish a roommate agreement to outline expectations.
- **Accessory Dwelling Units (ADUs)**: Build or renovate an ADU, such as a basement apartment or a detached guesthouse. Rent it out for additional income.
- **Live-In Flips**: Purchase a fixer-upper, live in it while renovating, and sell it at a profit. This approach requires hands-on effort but can yield substantial returns.

- **Rental Space:** Lease parts of your property, such as garage space for storage or land for RV parking (Araj 2024).

Rental income from house hacking must be reported to the IRS (Araj 2024). Use Schedule E for real estate income, and if you offer additional services beyond property maintenance, you may owe self-employment tax.

I found one success story from house hacking quite inspiring. Andres Felipe Alba Hernandez's journey into house hacking began with a vision for both a home and an investment. He and his wife were looking for a place to settle down and start a family, and they found a perfect fit in a 5-bedroom, 2.5-bath home located in a desirable neighborhood. The area was known for its great schools and family-friendly atmosphere, making it the ideal spot to lay down roots. The price, $340,000, was fair for the location, and the home's layout was spacious enough to allow for creative use of its rooms.

With just $20,000 invested as a 5 percent down payment, Andres made a bold move into real estate. He financed the deal conventionally, but the decision was far from typical. Instead of using the house solely as a family home, he turned it into a house-hack. They moved into the main bedroom, transformed a small room on the first floor into his office, and rented out the remaining three bedrooms on Airbnb and Furnished Finder.

Initially, Andres had his doubts. The setup seemed unconventional—how would guests manage without a full kitchen? But as it turned out, demand came from an unexpected mix of travelers, students, and nurses, all seeking temporary accommodations. He set clear house rules—no cooking, but guests could use the microwave, toaster, and coffee maker—and that was enough to make the rental work. IIis worries about the house hack not succeeding quickly faded as the property became a source of steady income.

Andres's efforts paid off in more ways than one. Over the first two years, the property appreciated significantly, allowing him to remove his private mortgage insurance (PMI). As the value of the house continued to rise, he was able to tap into a $100,000 home equity line of credit, which he used to invest in further opportunities. The small trade-off of sharing their home with short-term renters turned out to be a smart investment decision, giving them a platform to grow their real estate portfolio (Bigger Pockets 2024).

Building Credit

In real estate, your credit score is the gatekeeper to many opportunities. It's a reflection of your financial reliability, meaning lenders use it to assess how likely you are to repay loans. A higher credit score can open doors to better loan offers, lower interest rates, and more favorable terms. In essence, it dictates your access to traditional financing. If you're aiming to secure a conventional mortgage or any other type of traditional loan, maintaining a strong credit score is very important. This score influences both the approval of your loan application and the interest rate you're offered. A higher score can save you thousands of dollars over the life of a loan by reducing your monthly payments. Lower rates mean less money paid out over time, freeing up funds for further investments.

Building a strong credit score does not rely on a secret formula, but following certain guidelines can help.

The most important step is paying your loans on time, every time. Setting up automatic payments or electronic reminders can assist in staying consistent. If you've missed payments, focus on getting current and maintaining timely repayments, as repayment history is a major factor in credit score calculations. Prioritize paying off high-interest credit cards and loans, as these debts can quickly spiral out of control.

It is also important to avoid nearing your credit limit. Credit scoring models assess how much of your available credit you are using, so keeping balances low compared to your total credit limit is key. Experts recommend using no more than 30 percent of your total credit limit (Consumer Financial Protection Bureau 2024). Closing credit card accounts and consolidating balances onto one card can negatively impact your score if it results in high credit utilization.

A longer credit history positively impacts your score, as it reflects your ability to manage credit accounts responsibly over time. Consistently paying loans as agreed with lenders provides a clearer picture of your reliability as a borrower. Additionally, apply for credit only when necessary. Frequent applications for credit in a short time frame can signal financial instability to lenders. Lastly, regularly check your credit reports for errors and dispute any inaccuracies. Keep an eye on old, unused credit card accounts to ensure they are not being misused by identity thieves. Following these practices can help you establish and maintain a strong credit profile.

In this chapter, we covered multiple financing avenues available for real estate investors, each offering unique benefits and considerations. From conventional loans with their steady terms to more dynamic options like hard money loans and crowdfunding, choosing the right path depends on your specific needs, timeline, and risk tolerance. By understanding these financing methods, you can make informed decisions that support their investment goals and contribute to their long-term success in the real estate market.

CHAPTER 4
MAKING THE DEAL

> *"Deals work best when each side gets something it wants from the other."*

—DONALD TRUMP

So, you have chosen the property you want to buy and have your finances improved. How can you make the deal? In this chapter, we're going to cover everything you need to know about closing the deal on a house. This will include gaining access to off-market deals through real estate professionals, creating a well-crafted offer, using negotiation tactics, and knowing what to expect in the closing process.

Building a Network

In real estate, who you know can be just as important as what you know. Building a wide network of real estate professionals will unlock opportunities that would otherwise remain hidden. A strong network grants you access to off-market deals, provides invaluable professional advice, and opens doors to partnerships and collaborations that can accelerate your investment journey. As we discussed in Chapter Two, off-market properties are those that are not publicly listed for sale, meaning they do not appear on the MLS or other widely accessible platforms. These properties can offer attractive investment opportunities because of reduced competition.

There are a range of real estate professionals who can make up your network. Real estate agents and brokers are your eyes and ears in the market, offering insights and alerts on properties that match your criteria. They often know about listings before they become public, giving you a competitive edge. Real estate attorneys can guarantee legal compliance and protect your interests through well-drafted contracts. Property inspectors provide a detailed assessment of a property's condition, highlighting potential issues that could affect its value.

You can build this network by attending local real estate meetups and networking events. These gatherings are fertile ground for meeting professionals who share your interests and can offer guidance. Join online real estate forums and groups, where discussions often lead to valuable insights and connections. Platforms like BiggerPockets or local Facebook groups can be excellent starting points. Don't hesitate to reach out to professionals for informational interviews. A simple coffee meeting can yield advice that could save you time and money. These interactions expand your network and deepen your understanding of the real estate landscape, making you a more informed and confident investor.

Crafting Winning Offers: Tips and Tricks

When venturing into real estate, crafting a winning offer isn't just about numbers; it's about making an impression in a competitive market. The right offer sets you apart, communicates your seriousness, and builds credibility with the seller. In a market where multiple bids are common, your offer needs to stand out—not just in price but in how it's presented and structured. Building credibility is essential. This means not just offering the right amount but doing so in a way that reassures the seller of your ability to close the deal efficiently and smoothly. A well-crafted offer can also secure favorable terms and conditions, which might include seller concessions or adjustments that add value beyond the purchase price.

Here's a detailed breakdown of the steps involved in making a purchase offer for a home:

1. Ensure Your Financing and Cash Are Ready

Before making an offer, make sure that your financing is in place. If you're not paying cash, obtaining a mortgage preapproval from at least one lender is good. Ideally, this preapproval should be obtained before you begin house hunting. It will provide you with a clear understanding of how much you're qualified to borrow, which helps you determine what you can afford. Additionally, it signals to the seller that you're financially capable of making the purchase.

If you're preapproved for more than what the property is listed for, you might want to request a customized preapproval letter for a lower amount so that you demonstrate your ability to secure financing without revealing your maximum borrowing capacity, which could influence the seller's counteroffer.

Also, make sure that the cash you'll need for the down payment, earnest money deposit, and closing costs is available in your checking or savings account and ready to be accessed. If you need to transfer funds from investments or between different accounts, make sure to allow enough time for these transactions to settle before you need the money (Wood 2024).

2. Clarify How Your Buyer's Agent Gets Paid

On August 17, 2024, new regulations came into effect following an antitrust lawsuit settlement with the National Association of Realtors (NAR) (Wood 2024). If you're working with a real estate agent, you will need to sign a contract with them before submitting an offer. This contract, often called a buyer representation agreement, outlines how your agent will be compensated. Historically, the seller paid the agent's commission, which was typically split between the buyer's and seller's agents. However, with the new rules, your buyer's agent may charge a flat fee or an hourly rate, and you may need to negotiate who—buyer or seller—will cover the buyer's agent's fees.

3. Set an Offer Price

Your real estate agent can help you determine a competitive offer price by conducting a comparative market analysis, as we discussed in Chapter Two. This analysis compares the prices of similar homes that have recently sold in the area. Whether you offer above or below the listing price depends on various factors, such as the market conditions (buyer's market vs. seller's market) and the specific condition of the property.

In a seller's market, buyers often offer above the listing price, but this may not always be necessary, especially if the property needs significant repairs or has been on the market for a while. Keep your budget in mind when setting an offer price, making sure that it's something you can afford, regardless of market conditions (Wood 2024).

4. Decide on the Earnest Money to Offer

Earnest money is a deposit made to show the seller you're serious about the purchase. This money is usually held in escrow and can later be applied to your down payment at closing. If you back out of the deal for reasons not specified in the offer, the seller can keep the earnest money. However, if the deal falls through because of the seller's actions (e.g., accepting a higher offer after agreeing to yours), the earnest money should be returned.

Typically, earnest money amounts range from 1 percent to 3 percent of the home's price (Wood 2024). Offering a larger amount may help your offer stand out in competitive markets.

5. Select Your Contingencies

Contingencies are clauses that allow you to cancel the contract under certain circumstances, usually without forfeiting your earnest money. Common contingencies include:

- **Final Loan Approval**: Guarantees that you can back out of the deal if your mortgage isn't approved within a certain timeframe.

- **Home Inspection**: Allows you to negotiate repairs, ask for a price reduction, or walk away from the deal if significant issues are discovered during the inspection.
- **Appraisal**: Protects you if the property appraises for less than the agreed-upon price, which may affect your financing (Wood 2024).

Consult your real estate agent about which contingencies to include, as well as the risks of waiving any of them. While contingencies protect your interests, they can also make your offer less appealing in competitive markets.

6. *Write the Purchase Offer*

Typically, your real estate agent will write the purchase offer using a residential purchase agreement tailored to your needs and compliant with local laws. Once signed by both parties, this agreement becomes a legally binding contract.

The purchase agreement generally includes:

- **Address**: The legal address of the property.
- **Price**: The agreed-upon purchase price.
- **Earnest Money**: The amount of earnest money and conditions for its use.
- **Offer Expiration**: The deadline for the seller to accept the offer is usually one or two days in most markets.
- **Fixtures and Personal Property**: Items included with the property, such as appliances or lighting fixtures.
- **Escrow**: The name of the title company handling escrow.
- **Title**: The requirement for the seller to provide a clear title.

- **Contingencies**: Clauses protecting the buyer's interests.
- **Seller Disclosures**: The seller must provide the required information about the property.
- **Closing Date**: The anticipated date for closing, typically thirty to sixty days after the offer acceptance.
- **Closing Costs**: Which party (buyer or seller) is responsible for certain costs and taxes, including any negotiated seller contributions?
- **Broker's Fees**: Details about who will pay the broker's commission.
- **Walk-through Inspection**: The right to inspect the property prior to closing.
- **Delivery of Possession**: Specifies when the seller must vacate and turn over the keys (Wood 2024).

Some buyers choose to submit a personal letter to the seller to emotionally appeal to them. A heartfelt letter to the seller can make a significant impact. It's an opportunity to connect emotionally, sharing your intentions for the property and why it matters to you. This simple gesture can make your offer memorable. However, this is not legally binding and may not be effective, particularly if it leads to discrimination (Wood 2024).

7. *Walk Away, Negotiate, or Proceed to Closing*

After reviewing your offer, the seller can accept, counter, or reject it:

- **Accepted Offer**: Once the seller accepts the offer, both parties must sign the agreement for it to become legally binding. At this point, you can proceed with finalizing your mortgage application and begin the closing process.

- **Counteroffer**: If the seller counters, you can either accept it and continue with the process or submit your own counteroffer. Negotiations may continue until both parties agree on the terms.
- **Rejected Offer**: If the seller rejects your offer, you may feel disappointed. But remember the growth mindset that we discussed in chapter one. You should regroup with your agent to explore other homes and refine your strategy.

Mastering Negotiation Tactics for Better Deals

In real estate, the ability to negotiate effectively can make the difference between an average deal and a profitable one. It's about securing terms and conditions that maximize your returns. By reducing the purchase price, you immediately increase your equity and potential for profit. Favorable terms might include seller concessions or extended closing dates, each adding layers of value to your purchase. But beyond financial gain, negotiation is about building relationships. Creating win-win situations creates goodwill, paving the way for future opportunities and collaborations.

Negotiation is a two-way street, and there are several aspects of the property transaction where you can be flexible to achieve a more favorable price. You may have the opportunity to negotiate on the length of the settlement period, the amount of deposit required, conditions regarding existing tenants or vacant possession, and any fixtures or inclusions. These elements can be used strategically to your advantage, depending on the situation. Before entering negotiations, prepare a list of non-negotiables and potential concessions. Knowing your limits prevents you from making impulsive decisions. Consider what you're willing to compromise on and what you aren't.

Now, let's dive into the tactics that can help you seal the deal. Begin with anchoring, a technique where you set the initial offer to establish a starting point. This tactic shapes the negotiation's framework, guiding subsequent discussions. Silence is another powerful tool. After making an offer, resist the urge to fill the silence with justifications. This pause puts pressure on the other party to respond, often revealing their true position. Knowing when to walk away is equally important. Sometimes, the best deal is the one you don't make. Leverage market data and comparables to strengthen your position. Presenting hard facts about property values and market trends adds credibility to your offer. Researching the seller's motivations and needs can help you understand why they're selling, which can provide leverage. For instance, a seller eager to close quickly might accept a lower offer if it ensures a fast transaction. Building rapport with the seller is the final piece. Establishing trust and mutual respect can lead to more favorable terms, as sellers are often more willing to negotiate with someone they like and trust (Macquarie Bank n.d.).

The Closing Process: What to Expect and How to Prepare

Once the seller accepts your offer, the closing process will begin. As you approach the closing process, it's important to understand what this phase entails and why it holds such significance. Closing is the final step when the property officially changes hands. It begins with finalizing the purchase agreement. Next comes the title search and insurance. A title search verifies that the seller has the legal right to sell the property and that there are no outstanding claims against it. Title insurance protects you from potential disputes over ownership. Property appraisal and inspection follow, which are essential to confirm that the property's value aligns with the agreed purchase price and that its condition is as expected. Finally, there are closing costs and fees, which can include loan origination fees, attorney fees, and taxes. These must be settled to finalize the transaction (Downey 2024).

At the closing table, you will encounter several key documents, including:

1. **Closing Disclosure or Statement**: This document is required by federal law and outlines all costs associated with the property purchase, such as loan fees, real estate taxes, and other related expenses.
2. **Promissory Note**: This document specifies the loan amount, interest rate, payment schedule, and term length, as well as the penalties the lender can impose if the borrower defaults on the loan.
3. **Deed of Trust**: Also known as a mortgage in some states, this document acts as a security instrument, pledging the property as collateral for the loan.
4. **Deed or Title Transfer Document**: This document is necessary to officially transfer property ownership to the buyer.
5. **Notice of Right to Cancel**: This notice provides a three-day window for borrowers to cancel the mortgage loan. Once the documents are signed at closing, however, you no longer have the right to cancel if purchasing with a mortgage loan (Downey 2024).

A closing protection letter (CPL) is a contract between a title insurance underwriter and a lender. It ensures that the lender is indemnified against actual losses caused by certain types of misconduct by the closing agent. Title underwriters authorize closing agents to issue these letters when the closing agent is expected to issue the underwriter's title insurance policies for the transaction. These letters usually make the borrower a third-party beneficiary in the purchase transaction. Common provisions include failure to follow closing instructions, fraud or dishonesty in handling funds or documents, and issues related to the validity or effectiveness of documents needed for the loan (Downey 2024).

A closing disclosure is a five-page form required by federal law that summarizes the mortgage details. This document outlines your loan terms, monthly payments, interest rates, and any fees associated with the loan. You must receive this form at least three days before closing, allowing you to review the details before finalizing the transaction (Downey 2024).

It's important to carefully review all closing documents for accuracy. Double-check loan terms, interest rates, and the loan amount, as well as personal information such as your name and address. If you spot any errors, contact your lender immediately to have them corrected. Request to see documents in advance to ensure everything is accurate before signing.

Generally, you can move into your new property immediately after closing. However, some buyers may request earlier possession, which would require the seller to accept the risk that the buyer's financing may not be approved. In other instances, possession may be delayed until a later date than the closing itself.

In this chapter, we covered the importance of building a strong network in real estate and the essential steps to crafting a successful purchase offer. By connecting with industry professionals, such as real estate agents, brokers, attorneys, and inspectors, you gain valuable insights and access to exclusive opportunities, such as off-market deals. We also explored the main elements of making an effective offer, including making sure your financing is in place, determining a competitive price, offering earnest money, selecting contingencies, and negotiating terms. Furthermore, we discussed the closing process, highlighting the necessary documentation and the steps for a smooth transition of property ownership.

Lastly, one of the best things you can do on your real estate journey is to find at least three mentors who can guide you through different aspects of investing. Don't just wait for the right mentor to appear—be intentional about who you seek out. Write down the qualities and expertise you want in each mentor, whether it's experience in financing, property management, or negotiating deals. Look for people who have walked the path you want to take, and don't be afraid to reach out, ask questions, and build relationships. The right mentors can accelerate your success and help you avoid costly mistakes!

If you're finding this book helpful, I'd really appreciate it if you could leave a review on Amazon or Goodreads. Your feedback helps others discover these strategies and keeps me motivated to share more investing insights! Thank you, Chad ☺

CHAPTER 5

MANAGING YOUR PROPERTIES

"Real estate is like Jack and the Beanstalk's goose that lays golden eggs. It's something that pays you month after month, whether you are working or not."

— KATHY FETTKE

Congratulations—by this point, you have your first property. But now the real work begins—managing your property effectively to guarantee it remains a valuable asset in your portfolio. A well-managed property not only retains its value but also appreciates over time, making your investment even more rewarding. Let's delve into the role of a property manager and explore the strategies that can transform your property into a thriving, income-generating asset.

At the heart of property management lies a set of responsibilities that ensure both the property and its tenants are well taken care of. These can be summarized as property management, tenant management, and financial administration.

Property Management

Property management encompasses a broad range of responsibilities. One of the primary duties of a landlord is making sure that the property remains habitable and safe for tenants. Routine property inspections and preventive maintenance are essential components of effective property management. Maintaining the property's functionality and addressing small issues before they become larger problems will help protect the investment and ensure tenants are satisfied.

Effective property management brings a host of benefits that ripple through every aspect of your investment. One of the most significant advantages is higher tenant retention rates. When tenants are satisfied with their living conditions and management, they are more likely to stay long-term, reducing turnover and associated costs. Reduced vacancies mean a steadier income stream and less time spent on marketing and tenant acquisition. Moreover, good management improves the property's condition over time. Regular maintenance and timely repairs prevent minor issues from becoming major problems, preserving the property's value and appeal (Luxon 2023).

Handling Maintenance and Repairs Efficiently

Routine inspections are necessary to assess the condition of your property and ensure everything is in working order. Many landlords schedule inspections every six to twelve months to check for maintenance needs and to document the property's condition. It's important to notify tenants in advance of any inspections and be respectful of their space.

To handle maintenance efficiently, start by creating a detailed maintenance schedule. This schedule should outline regular checks and servicing of essential systems, such as heating, ventilation, air conditioning (HVAC), plumbing, and electrical systems. Regularly scheduled inspections help catch minor issues before they become major problems. Prioritizing urgent repairs is also important. When a tenant reports a leaky faucet or a faulty lock, addressing these issues promptly prevents further damage and shows tenants that their comfort and safety are your priority.

Keeping detailed maintenance records is another good practice. These records track the history of repairs and upgrades, providing valuable insights into recurring issues and helping you plan future maintenance more effectively. They also serve as a transparent way to communicate with tenants about the work being done.

The role of professional contractors cannot be overstated when it comes to property maintenance. Reliable contractors bring expertise and efficiency to the table so that repairs are done correctly and swiftly. Building long-term relationships with contractors is beneficial. Familiarity with your property and its history can lead to more efficient service and potentially better pricing.

It is important to distinguish between wear and tear and damage when maintaining a rental property. Wear and tear refers to the natural deterioration that occurs due to regular use, such as faded paint, worn carpet, or minor scuffs on walls. These are expected and not the responsibility of the tenant. Damage, however, is the result of misuse or neglect, such as a broken window or holes in the wall, which should be the tenant's responsibility (Luxon 2023).

Adding Value to Your Properties: Renovations and Upgrades

Another important distinction is the difference between repairs and property improvements. Repairs are necessary to maintain the habitability of the property, such as fixing leaks or replacing faulty appliances. Property improvements, on the other hand, increase the value of the property, such as remodeling a kitchen or adding a new patio. The cost of repairs can often be deducted from the tenant's security deposit if they are found responsible for the damage, but improvements are generally not included.

Imagine walking through your rental property, envisioning its potential to attract higher-paying tenants and increase in value. Strategic renovations and upgrades can unlock this potential. By investing in improvements, you can not only enhance the property's appeal but also its market value. Higher-paying tenants often seek modern, well-maintained properties, and by delivering this standard, you attract those willing to pay a premium for comfort and style. Moreover, properties that boast recent upgrades are more likely to appreciate over time, ensuring that your investment grows alongside your rental income.

One of the most impactful areas to focus on is the kitchen. Modernizing this space can significantly boost your property's value and desirability. Installing energy-efficient appliances both draws eco-conscious tenants and reduces long-term utility costs. Bathrooms, too, offer great potential for value addition. Simple changes like updating fixtures, adding a fresh coat of paint, or installing new vanities can make a substantial difference. These improvements create a sense of luxury and cleanliness that many renters find irresistible. Flooring upgrades are another avenue to explore. Hardwood or laminate floors are popular choices due to their durability and aesthetic appeal. They are easy to maintain and create a cohesive, polished look throughout the property. Enhanced lighting fixtures can also transform a space, adding warmth and sophistication.

Curb appeal is the first impression your property makes and is beneficial for attracting tenants. Investing in landscaping can dramatically enhance this aspect. Simple additions like planting shrubs, installing a new walkway, or adding outdoor lighting can elevate your property's exterior. These changes, while seemingly minor, can have a big impact on tenant perception and, ultimately, rental decisions (Luxon 2023).

Tenant Management

The second aspect of property management is related to the tenants. Tenant management can be one of the most challenging aspects of being a landlord. While many investors focus on maximizing profits and managing finances, the reality of tenant interactions often involves dealing with complaints, chasing late rent, and handling unexpected maintenance emergencies. Despite these challenges, tenants are the customers of your rental business, and like any business, it is vital to maintain a professional yet supportive relationship with them. Happy tenants lead to long-term, stable rentals with fewer vacancies, which directly contributes to your investment's financial success (Luxon 2023).

Creating an Attractive Rental Listing

The process of tenant management begins long before you sign a lease. The first interaction potential tenants have with your property is often the rental listing. An effective listing can generate interest and help you attract the right tenants. A well-crafted rental listing includes all the relevant details about the property: square footage, number of bedrooms and bathrooms, rent price, amenities, and any special features. High-quality photos of the property significantly increase the likelihood of tenants expressing interest (Luxon 2023). These should be taken during the day with good natural light to showcase the property at its best.

It's also important to consider the neighborhood when creating a listing. Highlight nearby schools, parks, public transport options, and shopping centers. The more detailed and accurate your listing is, the better. Providing too little information or misrepresenting the property can lead to confusion, wasted time, and frustration for both you and potential tenants. For example, claiming that there is ample parking when only a small number of spots are available can create tension once tenants arrive.

Screening Tenants

Once you start receiving inquiries, the next step is the tenant screening process. Screening potential tenants properly is vital for finding tenants who will respect your property and pay rent on time. This process involves reviewing tenant applications, running background checks, evaluating credit scores, and checking rental histories. These steps help you identify tenants with a proven track record of responsible behavior.

As you move forward with screening, make sure that you are following fair housing laws. We'll look at this in detail later in the chapter. But for now, know that the Fair Housing Act prohibits discrimination based on race, color, religion, gender, familial status, or disability, among other factors (McCall 2024). Using standardized criteria during the tenant selection process and applying them consistently is necessary to avoid legal issues and make sure that every applicant is treated fairly.

Retaining Tenants

Retaining good tenants is just as important as finding them. Building positive relationships with tenants is the foundation of retention.

Good communication is at the heart of effective tenant management. Establishing clear and efficient communication channels can help resolve issues quickly and prevent misunderstandings. While some landlords prefer to communicate via phone calls or email, using a tenant portal can streamline this process. A digital platform allows tenants to submit maintenance requests, pay rent, and receive notices about inspections, repairs, or changes in the rental agreement. It also keeps all communication organized and easily accessible.

Setting expectations upfront about how and when you prefer to be contacted will make communication smoother. Additionally, be responsive to your tenants' concerns and inquiries. Tenants who feel heard and respected are more likely to remain content throughout their tenancy, which can lead to longer lease terms and fewer vacancies.

Understanding Landlord-Tenant Laws

Landlord-tenant law governs the rights and responsibilities of both landlords and tenants in relation to rental properties.

A lease agreement serves as the foundational document that defines the landlord-tenant relationship. It specifies the rights and obligations of both parties and establishes the terms under which the tenant is allowed to occupy the rental property. Although some states recognize oral agreements, a written lease agreement is always the best practice for formalizing the arrangement. Not only does it provide clarity, but it also offers legal protection should any disputes arise. A rental agreement typically refers to shorter-term arrangements, such as a month-to-month lease, whereas a lease agreement generally refers to longer-term commitments, often lasting at least one year (McCall 2024).

A well-crafted lease agreement should leave no ambiguity about the expectations and responsibilities of both parties. The clarity of such a document helps prevent conflicts and misunderstandings, ensuring that both the landlord and tenant have a shared understanding of their duties and rights.

While the specifics of a lease can vary based on the location and type of rental, certain provisions are commonly found in most lease and rental agreements. These provisions serve to define the parameters of the agreement and ensure that both parties are on the same page. Some standard clauses include:

1. **Identification of the Lessor and Lessee**: The lease must clearly state the names of both the landlord (lessor) and the tenant (lessee). This ensures that both parties are properly identified and legally bound by the agreement.
2. **Property Address and Legal Description**: The lease should include the full address of the rental unit, as well as any legal descriptions that may apply, to ensure there is no confusion about the property in question.
3. **Contact Information for the Landlord or Property Manager**: This clause ensures that the tenant has a point

of contact for any issues or inquiries that may arise during their tenancy.

4. **Term of the Lease**: This specifies the duration of the lease or rental agreement. For standard leases, the term is usually one year, but rental agreements, such as month-to-month leases, are more flexible and are often used for shorter arrangements.

5. **Rent Amount and Payment Due Date**: The lease should clearly specify how much rent is due, when it's due (e.g., on the 1st of each month), and any penalties for late payments. This provides transparency and helps avoid confusion regarding payment expectations.

6. **Late Fees**: Many leases include a provision for late fees if rent is not paid on time. These fees should be clearly outlined, including the amount and the grace period for late payments.

7. **Security Deposit**: Most landlords require a security deposit before a tenant moves in. This deposit serves as financial protection for the landlord in case of property damage or unpaid rent. The lease agreement should specify the amount of the deposit and the conditions under which it may be withheld.

8. **Occupancy and Roommates**: The lease may set limits on the number of people who can occupy the rental unit. This helps the landlord maintain control over who is living in the property and ensures that it complies with local zoning laws.

9. **Subletting**: Some leases prohibit subletting the rental unit, while others may allow it with prior approval. This clause helps the landlord maintain control over who occupies their property (McCall 2024).

Landlord Responsibilities

A lease agreement should outline the landlord's responsibilities, making sure that they fulfill their obligations to maintain a safe and habitable living environment for the tenant. A few fundamental duties that should be included in the lease are:

1. **Performing Necessary Repairs**: The landlord is responsible for making necessary repairs to the property. This includes addressing issues such as plumbing, heating, or electrical problems. The lease should specify how the landlord will handle repair requests and the timeframe in which repairs will be made.
2. **Maintaining Common Areas**: If the rental property includes shared spaces, such as hallways, stairwells, or laundry facilities, the landlord is responsible for ensuring these areas are well-maintained and safe for tenants.
3. **Upkeeping the Property**: The landlord is required to maintain the property in a condition that meets health and safety standards. This can include addressing issues such as pest control, mold, and the overall cleanliness of the rental unit.
4. **Notice Before Entering**: The lease should specify the notice period the landlord must give before entering the rental property. In most cases, landlords are required to provide at least 24 hours notice before entering the property, except in cases of emergency (McCall 2024).

If any disputes arise during the term of the lease, both parties should refer to the written agreement. As a binding contract, the lease provides clear guidance on how to handle issues and ensures that the landlord and tenant understand their rights and obligations.

A security deposit is a common requirement for landlords, providing a safety net for potential damages or unpaid rent at the end of the lease term. While the amount can vary, state laws typically impose limits on how much a landlord can charge. For instance, in California, the security deposit cannot exceed two months' rent for an unfurnished property or three months' rent for a furnished property (McCall 2024).

It's important to differentiate between a security deposit and last month's rent. The security deposit is intended to cover damages or other charges at the end of the lease, whereas last month's rent is simply a prepayment for the final month of the lease term.

To avoid disputes, the lease agreement should clearly state the conditions under which the security deposit can be withheld. This typically includes damage to the property beyond normal wear and tear, unpaid rent, or cleaning costs. Tenants should document the property's condition at move-in with photographs or a video to ensure that there is a clear record of the property's state before they move in.

Local and state laws also govern the timeframe in which the landlord must return the security deposit. In most cases, landlords are required to return the deposit within a certain number of days after the lease ends, minus any deductions for damages or unpaid rent. Understanding these legal requirements can help both parties avoid unnecessary conflicts.

Tenant Rights

As we mentioned above, the Fair Housing Act protects tenants from discrimination based on certain factors, including:

- Race
- Color
- Religion
- National origin
- Gender
- Disability
- Age
- Familial status (with exceptions for senior housing) (McCall 2024).

In addition to these federally protected rights, tenants also have several other important rights under the lease agreement. These include:

1. **The Right to Privacy**: Landlords must respect the tenant's privacy and cannot enter the rental unit without proper notice, except in emergency situations.
2. **The Right to Quiet Enjoyment**: Tenants have the right to live in the rental property without undue disturbances or interference from the landlord or other tenants.
3. **The Right to Safe and Livable Conditions**: Landlords are required to provide tenants with a safe and habitable living space. This includes maintaining the property and addressing issues that could compromise the tenant's health or safety.

4. **Protection from Environmental Hazards**: Tenants are entitled to live in a property free of lead poisoning, mold, or other environmental hazards (McCall 2024).

While tenants have certain rights, landlords also have legal rights that are designed to protect their investment. These rights include:

- **Eviction for Cause**: If a tenant fails to pay rent or violates the terms of the lease, the landlord has the right to evict them. However, eviction must follow the proper legal process, and landlords are prohibited from using self-help methods, such as forcibly removing a tenant's belongings.
- **Written Notice for Eviction**: In most cases, landlords must provide written notice of eviction and follow local laws regarding notice periods. If a tenant is being evicted for nonpayment of rent, landlords may need to provide the tenant with a grace period before initiating the eviction process.
- **Foreclosure Notification**: If the landlord's property is in foreclosure, they are typically required to notify tenants of the situation. Depending on local laws, tenants may have specific rights in the case of foreclosure, such as the right to remain in the property until the lease term ends (McCall 2024).

Financial Management

Finally, the third aspect of property management is financial management. Keeping track of income and expenses is important for making sure your property remains profitable. By maintaining accurate records of all rental income and expenses, you can assess the financial health of your property and identify areas where you can reduce costs or improve profitability.

Real estate investment software, such as Landlord Studio, can automate many aspects of financial management, such as tracking rent payments, logging maintenance costs, and generating tax reports. This software can simplify your bookkeeping and allow you to focus on growing your business. It also helps make sure that you don't miss any important deductions during tax season. One of the key benefits of using such software is the ability to collect rent online. Instead of dealing with checks or cash, tenants can make payments electronically, which ensures promptness and reduces the risk of late payments. This streamlined process not only improves cash flow but also simplifies bookkeeping, as all transactions are recorded automatically (Luxon 2023).

Managing maintenance requests is another area where property management software shines. Tenants can submit requests through the platform, and landlords can track the status of each request in real time. This transparency ensures that issues are addressed promptly, enhancing tenant satisfaction and reducing the likelihood of minor problems escalating into costly repairs. Moreover, these platforms help keep tenant records organized. Important documents like leases, payment histories, and maintenance logs are stored digitally, making them easily accessible whenever needed. This reduces the clutter of paperwork and ensures that the important information is always at your fingertips. (Luxon 2023)

In this chapter, we explored three key aspects of managing a rental property: property management, tenant management, and financial management. Property management involves staying on top of maintenance and ensuring the property is safe and well-kept. Tenant management focuses on building good relationships with tenants, sticking to lease agreements, and following legal requirements. Finally, financial management is all about keeping track of income and expenses, making sure you're staying profitable.

CHAPTER 6

MAXIMIZING CASH FLOW

"Real estate investing, even on a very small scale, remains a tried-and-true means of building an individual's cash flow and wealth."

— ROBERT KIYOSAKI

Now that you have a clear understanding of your responsibilities as a property owner, it's time to focus on strategies for maximizing cash flow. In this chapter, we will explore methods for determining the optimal rental rate that attracts quality tenants while ensuring profitability. We will also discuss ways to reduce vacancy periods, cut unnecessary expenses, and take advantage of tax benefits available to landlords. Implementing these strategies effectively can help you maintain a steady stream of income while optimizing the financial performance of your property.

Determining Ideal Rental Rate

To determine the ideal rental rate for your property, there are three things you need to consider: the market, your property, and your expenses.

First, look at the market. This involves examining similar properties in your area to understand what the going rates are. Look at properties with comparable sizes, amenities, and locations to gauge where your property stands. This analysis will provide a clear picture of the competitive landscape, allowing you to position your property effectively. Additionally, it's important to stay attuned to market conditions and adjust rental rates accordingly. Economic changes, such as shifts in employment rates or local developments, can impact rental demand.

Online rental rate tools and calculators can further assist in this process by offering data-driven insights into pricing trends. These tools analyze market data and suggest optimal rental pricing based on current demand and supply conditions, helping you avoid guesswork and base your decisions on solid information.

Second, look at your property's features and amenities. Unique features such as modern appliances, additional storage, or proximity to public transportation can justify higher rates. These amenities add value for tenants, enhancing their living experience and allowing you to command a premium price.

Third, look at your expenses. This includes all costs associated with owning and managing your property, such as mortgage payments, taxes, insurance, maintenance, and any other related expenses. Once you have a clear understanding of these costs, you can begin calculating the rent needed to cover them. Add up all your expenses and divide the total by twelve to find the minimum rent you need to charge each month to cover the basics.

It's important to recognize that you may not be able to cover every single expense through rent alone. While your investment is meant to generate profit in the long term, the local market conditions will primarily determine your property's rental price, influenced by the principles of supply and demand. If your property is located in a desirable area or has unique features, you may be able to charge a premium above the minimum.

In saying that, you should avoid the temptation to set rent too high. The impact of rental rate adjustments extends beyond immediate cash flow. Over time, aligning your rates with market conditions can lead to increased tenant retention. Tenants appreciate fair pricing and are more likely to renew leases if they feel they're receiving good value. This stability reduces turnover costs and vacancy periods, contributing to a healthier bottom line.

Reducing Vacancy Rates: Tips and Techniques

High vacancy rates can severely impact your cash flow, as each unoccupied unit represents lost income. This absence of revenue can create a financial strain, as mortgage payments and maintenance costs do not pause when a tenant moves out. Moreover, filling these vacancies often incurs additional marketing and turnover expenses. Every time a property sits empty, you might need to spend on advertising, refreshing paint, or repairing minor damages left by previous tenants. These costs can add up quickly, chipping away at your profits and making it harder to achieve your financial goals (Sutton 2024).

So, the best approach to limiting vacancies and reducing the vacancy rate in rental properties is by focusing on long-term residents. Retaining quality tenants who consistently pay rent on time, maintain the property, and follow the lease terms is going to avoid the stress and cost associated with finding new residents. Rather than expending energy on finding new tenants, concentrate on keeping the good ones you already have.

First, create a positive move-in experience for new residents. First impressions have a significant impact on long-term satisfaction, and residents will remember how they were treated. To make the move-in process smoother, thoroughly clean the unit, provide utility and parking information, include rental insurance details, and make the contact information for property management readily available. Moving can be a stressful event, so making the transition as seamless as possible is an important first step. Additionally, offering a move-in package can go a long way in making tenants feel valued. Such packages might include an informational binder with utility details, parking regulations, rules of conduct, and maintenance request procedures. A small move-in kit with essentials like toilet paper, cleaning supplies, and air fresheners can also show thoughtful consideration. A simple welcome gift, such as a Starbucks gift card, can make a lasting impression and support a positive relationship between landlord and tenant.

The second step is addressing maintenance issues quickly. One of the most common reasons for lease non-renewal is a slow response to maintenance requests. A landlord should pay attention to any recurring issues that tenants raise. If multiple residents request similar improvements or amenities, assess the feasibility of meeting those needs. When a tenant decides not to renew, it is helpful to ask why they are leaving and what could have convinced them to stay. Understanding these reasons can help prevent future vacancies and resolve simple issues that may have influenced their decision (Sutton 2024).

When it comes to rent increases, you must carefully weigh the pros and cons. Raising rent can help keep properties competitive and align with market rates, but it can also drive tenants away, especially in a market where many people are already struggling with high costs of living. If you need to raise prices, try implementing small, gradual rent increases each year to avoid shocking tenants with significant hikes. This approach helps maintain long-term residents and reduces the risk of vacancies.

Reaching out about lease renewals early is also important. The sooner you contact tenants, the more likely they are to renew their leases. If a resident decides not to renew, you should have a clear system in place for handling the transition, including the return of keys, inspection of the unit, and proper documentation of any required notices.

In some cases, eviction may be necessary, which will inevitably result in a vacancy. However, you can regularly inspect the property during the eviction process and take possession of the unit as quickly as possible to minimize the vacancy period.

Lastly, refining your resident screening process is going to help you find well-qualified tenants, reducing the likelihood of future vacancies. Given the current market, it is advisable to look for applicants whose income is at least two to two and a half times the monthly rent (Sutton 2024).

If your property does become vacant, you can attract new tenants faster through effective marketing. For one, a well-maintained exterior invites prospective tenants and sets your property apart from others. Consider sprucing up the landscaping, adding a fresh coat of paint, or updating the entryway. These small improvements can make a significant difference in first impressions. Offering flexible lease terms can also appeal to a broader audience, accommodating various tenant needs and circumstances. For instance, providing options for short-term leases or allowing pets can widen your pool of potential renters. Move-in incentives, such as a reduced first month's rent or a free parking space, can be the nudge that turns a potential tenant into a confirmed one.

Expense Management: Cutting Costs Without Compromising Quality

Imagine your rental property as a well-oiled machine. Every part needs to work efficiently to ensure smooth operation and maximize profitability. Expense management is the maintenance that keeps this machine running at its best. Properly managing expenses will increase cash flow and enhance the profitability of your investment. By keeping expenses low, you improve your net income, which is the lifeblood of your real estate venture.

Regular maintenance is essential, but it doesn't have to break the bank. The most important thing to do is preventive maintenance, such as regular HVAC inspections or gutter cleaning, which can prevent costly repairs down the line. Although it can be tempting to put off fixing an issue, the longer you leave it, the bigger the problem will be later on. By addressing small issues before they escalate, you maintain the property's value and tenant satisfaction. Implement a routine maintenance schedule and stick to it. This proactive approach ensures the property remains in good condition, reducing the chance of unexpected expenses (Rent Better 2024).

Another good idea is energy-efficient upgrades, which are a smart way to cut costs without sacrificing quality. Simple changes, like installing LED lighting or energy-efficient appliances, can significantly reduce utility bills. These upgrades also make your property more attractive to environmentally conscious tenants.

Another strategy is negotiating service contracts with vendors. This can apply to landscaping, cleaning, or maintenance services. Establishing long-term relationships with service providers can lead to better rates and more reliable service. Don't shy away from discussing discounts or bundled services, as these can lead to considerable savings over time.

Budgeting and financial planning are the backbone of effective expense management. Start by tracking and categorizing all expenses. Use software or a simple spreadsheet to record every outlay, from minor repairs to major renovations. This detailed record-keeping will help you identify areas for cost savings. Look for patterns or spikes in spending that might indicate inefficiencies. Once you have a clear picture of your expenses, set financial goals and monitor your progress. You can also take advantage of the technology available, such as RentBetter, which will help you to monitor finances effectively.

Leveraging Tax Benefits and Deductions

When you own a rental property, you can write off expenses related to its operation, maintenance, and management. Common deductions include property taxes, insurance premiums, mortgage interest, property management fees, and repair costs. Additionally, you can also deduct certain expenses tied to running your real estate investment business, such as advertising, office space, business equipment (like computers or stationery), legal and accounting fees, and travel expenses. These deductions lower your taxable income, which can result in tax savings. For example, if your rental income is $25,000 and your qualified expenses total $8,000, your taxable income from the real estate business would be reduced to $17,000. It's important to keep accurate records and receipts for all claimed expenses to ensure you can support your deductions in case of an IRS audit (Gariepy 2024).

Another important tax advantage for real estate investors is depreciation. Depreciation accounts for the gradual loss in value of a property over time, typically due to wear and tear. As a real estate investor, you can deduct depreciation on income-producing rental properties. The IRS allows you to deduct depreciation over a period of 27.5 years for residential properties and 39 years for commercial properties. For instance, if you buy a property worth $300,000 and plan to rent it out, you can deduct $10,909 annually as depreciation (calculated by dividing the building's value by 27.5 years). However, be aware that when you sell the property, you may be required to pay taxes on the depreciation deductions you've previously claimed. This process, known as depreciation recapture, means you could face higher taxes when selling the property, especially if the sale price exceeds the depreciated value. Tax strategies, such as a 1031 exchange, may help you defer depreciation recapture taxes (Gariepy 2024).

Real estate investors can also benefit from the pass-through deduction. If you own rental property through a sole proprietorship, partnership, LLC, or S Corporation, you may be able to deduct up to 20 percent of your qualified business income (QBI) on your personal tax return. For example, if you operate an LLC that owns rental properties and you receive $30,000 in rental income, you could deduct up to $6,000 from your taxable income. Keep in mind that specific rules and limitations apply, so it's important to consult with an accountant. This deduction, along with other provisions of the Tax Cut and Jobs Act of 2017, is set to expire in December 2025 (Gariepy 2024).

When you sell a property, capital gains tax may apply to any profits from the sale. There are two types of capital gains tax: short-term and long-term. Short-term capital gains apply if you sell a property within a year of owning it, and the profits are taxed at the same rate as ordinary income. This can result in a higher tax bill, as your total income (from both your salary and property sale) will be taxed together. Long-term capital gains, however, apply when you sell a property you've held for over a year. These gains are taxed at a lower rate than ordinary income, and in some cases, if your income is below a certain threshold, you may not have to pay any capital gains tax at all. For example, a married couple with a combined income of $75,000 may not owe any tax on long-term capital gains, as their tax bracket could be 0 percent (Gariepy 2024).

There are also opportunities to defer taxes through programs such as the 1031 exchange and opportunity zones. The 1031 exchange allows you to defer capital gains taxes by reinvesting the proceeds from the sale of one property into another property of equal or greater value. This tax-deferral strategy can be used indefinitely, but when you eventually sell the new property, you will be required to pay taxes on the deferred capital gains. Opportunity zones, designated by the U.S. Department of the Treasury, encourage investment in economically disadvantaged areas by offering tax incentives. Investors who reinvest capital gains into qualified opportunity funds can defer taxes, and if they hold the investment for a certain period, they may even avoid paying capital gains taxes altogether after ten years (Gariepy 2024).

Additionally, owning a rental property can help you avoid the FICA tax, which is generally required for self-employed individuals. The FICA tax, which covers Social Security and Medicare, typically requires you to pay both the employer and employee portion of the tax. However, rental income is not considered earned income, so property owners are not subject to the FICA tax. This can result in significant savings, especially if rental property is your primary source of income (Gariepy 2024).

In this chapter, you've explored strategies to maximize cash flow, from setting optimal rental rates to leveraging tax benefits. Each element plays a role in enhancing your property's profitability and resilience. As you move forward, remember that efficient financial management is key to sustaining and growing your investment.

CHAPTER 7
RISK MANAGEMENT

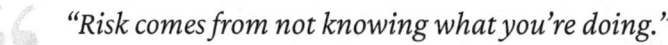 *"Risk comes from not knowing what you're doing."*

— WARREN BUFFETT

T he real estate market, much like the tides of an ocean, ebbs and flows. These fluctuations can significantly impact property values and rental income, affecting the stability of your investments. Understanding the underlying market cycles is, therefore, very important. Typically, these cycles consist of four phases: recovery, expansion, hypersupply, and recession (Rhode 2024). Recognizing where the market stands within these phases allows you to strategize accordingly. For instance, during the expansion phase, property values and demand rise, making it an opportune time for selling or increasing rents. Conversely, in a recession, prices may stagnate or fall, requiring a more conservative approach. Early warning signs, such as shifts in employment rates or changes in consumer spending, can signal upcoming market changes. By keeping a close eye on these indicators, you can anticipate shifts and adjust your strategies to protect your investments.

In general, there are a few ways to protect yourself against the unpredictable nature of the market. These include insurance, diversifying your portfolio, and building a contingency fund.

Protecting Your Investments with Insurance

Insurance can serve as a protective barrier that guards against the unpredictable nature of life. Think of it as a safety net that not only covers property damage and loss but also offers liability protection, ensuring that unexpected events don't derail your financial planning. When a storm hits, shingles fly off the roof, or a tenant trips on a loose step, insurance is there to cushion the blow. It provides peace of mind, knowing that the weight of financial loss is lessened because you have prepared for the unexpected.

Landlord Insurance

Landlord insurance is an essential protection for property owners who rent out their homes or other types of real estate. Unlike a standard homeowner's insurance policy, which typically covers a primary residence, landlord insurance is tailored to the unique risks associated with rental properties. It provides a range of coverage options that can help protect a landlord from financial losses (Rhode 2024).

One of the most important types of coverage offered by landlord insurance is liability coverage. This protects landlords if someone is injured on their rental property and decides to file a lawsuit. The costs associated with a personal injury claim can be extensive, covering things like medical expenses, lost wages, emotional distress, funeral costs, and legal fees. For instance, if a tenant or visitor is injured due to a faulty staircase or slip-and-fall accident, liability coverage can help cover the costs of the lawsuit and related expenses, which can be financially burdensome without insurance (Rhode 2024).

Another key element of landlord insurance is property damage coverage. This protects landlords from damage to the property itself, whether it's from a fire, natural disaster, theft, or vandalism. If a rental home or its outbuildings, such as a detached garage or storage shed, is damaged, the landlord can file a claim to cover the repairs. This also extends to personal property used in the rental, such as kitchen appliances, furniture, or landscaping equipment. For example, if a washer and dryer are damaged in a fire or stolen, the landlord's policy may cover the cost of replacing these items. However, it's important to note that landlord insurance typically does not cover the tenant's personal belongings; tenants should have their own renter's insurance for that.

In addition to damage to the property itself, landlord insurance can provide coverage for loss of rental income. This type of coverage is beneficial if a property is rendered uninhabitable due to a covered event, like a fire or major flooding, and the tenant needs to temporarily relocate while repairs are made. If a landlord is unable to collect rent during this period, the insurance can compensate for the lost income. For instance, if a tenant pays $2,000 per month in rent and the property needs six weeks of repairs, the landlord may be eligible for compensation up to $3,000 minus the deductible. This ensures that the landlord does not face financial strain while the property is being fixed (Rhode 2024).

Some landlords also opt to enhance their protection by adding an umbrella policy. This extra layer of coverage goes beyond the limits of a standard landlord insurance policy, providing additional liability protection. It can be especially useful for landlords who own multiple properties or face higher liability risks. An umbrella policy can help cover large, unexpected costs that exceed the coverage limits of a standard policy, such as serious injury claims or lawsuits (Rhode 2024).

Limited Liability Company

Another strategy many landlords use to protect their real estate assets is establishing a limited liability company (LLC). An LLC is a legal business entity that owns the rental property, with the landlord acting as the business owner. This provides a level of protection for personal assets, as the LLC separates the owner's personal finances from those of the rental property. For example, if a tenant sues a landlord over an injury or property dispute, the lawsuit typically only affects the assets held within the LLC. This means that, in the event of a lawsuit, personal assets like a primary home or savings are not at risk. For instance, if a landlord owns three properties worth $250,000 each, and each is placed in a separate LLC, the potential liability is limited to the value of a single property rather than exposing all three to potential claims. This separation helps protect the landlord's broader financial interests from claims related to one specific property (Rhode 2024).

Diversifying Your Investment Portfolio

To prepare for potential downturns, you can build a diversified investment portfolio. Diversification spreads risk across various property types and locations, reducing the impact of localized market slumps. If one market falls, another might rise, keeping your overall returns steady. Diversification enhances long-term financial stability by ensuring you aren't overly reliant on a single income stream (MRI 2024).

You should consider investing in different property types, such as residential, commercial, and industrial. Residential properties, like single-family homes and apartments, often provide consistent cash flow and are generally easier to manage. Commercial properties, including office spaces and retail units, can offer higher returns but come with increased complexity and risk. Industrial properties, such as warehouses, provide stability and are often less affected by economic cycles (MRI 2024).

Expanding your portfolio geographically is another strategy. Different regions have unique economic drivers and market conditions. Investing in various locations can shield you from localized downturns and capitalize on growth in emerging markets (MRI 2024).

Additionally, alternative real estate investments like Real Estate Investment Trusts (REITs) and crowdfunding platforms offer avenues for diversification without the need for direct property management. These options allow you to invest in larger projects or portfolios, spreading risk and enhancing returns (MRI 2024).

Building a Contingency Fund: Planning for Unexpected Expenses

In the unpredictable world of real estate investing, having a contingency fund is like owning an umbrella on a rainy day. Imagine facing a sudden roof leak after a storm or discovering that your property has plumbing issues. These situations demand immediate financial attention. When a tenant unexpectedly moves out or fails to pay rent, the fund provides the necessary cushion, allowing you to continue meeting financial obligations without stress. Additionally, unforeseen legal expenses can arise, such as disputes or compliance issues, and having a reserve ensures you're prepared to address these challenges head-on.

Building a contingency fund involves disciplined financial planning. Start by setting aside a percentage of your rental income each month. A common benchmark is 5 percent to 10 percent of monthly rent, but this can be adjusted based on your property's specific needs and risk factors. A good target is to have enough in your emergency fund to cover three months of expenses (Money Smart 2024).

Automating contributions to the fund is a smart strategy. By setting up automatic transfers from your rental income account to a dedicated contingency fund, you get consistent growth without relying on manual deposits. Regularly reviewing and adjusting the fund amount is also important. As your portfolio grows or market conditions change, reassess your contingency needs and make necessary adjustments. This proactive approach keeps your fund aligned with your investment strategy and risk profile.

In conclusion, protecting your real estate investments involves implementing proactive strategies to navigate market fluctuations and any unexpected challenges. Understanding market cycles and adjusting your approach based on the current phase can help maximize returns and minimize risks. Whether the market is in expansion or recession, measures like landlord insurance, diversifying your portfolio and building a contingency fund provide important protection. Insurance covers unforeseen events, such as property damage or tenant injuries, that could otherwise cause significant financial strain. Diversification across different property types and locations helps shield against localized downturns while maintaining a contingency fund allows for quick response to unexpected expenses. These strategies, when combined, help safeguard your investments and maintain financial stability in the face of market volatility.

CHAPTER 8

SCALING YOUR PORTFOLIO - HOW ARE YOU FUNDING NOW AND AS YOU GROW?

"The key to financial freedom and great wealth is a person's ability or skill to convert earned income into passive income and/or portfolio income."

— SUZE ORMAN

Once you have your first investment property, you might be wondering how to grow from there. In this chapter, we're going to cover techniques for scaling your portfolio, including the BRRRR strategy and reinvesting profits. We will also look at how to manage multiple properties and provide some advice on knowing when to sell.

The BRRRR Strategy

If you're considering diving into real estate investment, you may have come across the Buy, Rehab, Rent, Refinance, Repeat (BRRRR) Method. This strategy is designed to help investors grow a portfolio of rental properties and can be a profitable way to enter the real estate market. However, like any investment approach, it comes with both opportunities and risks. Understanding how the BRRRR Method works and weighing its advantages and disadvantages is essential before deciding if it's the right strategy for your financial goals (Nowacki 2024).

The BRRRR Method is a real estate investment strategy that revolves around purchasing distressed properties, renovating them to increase their value, renting them out for steady cash flow, and then refinancing the property to pull out the equity. The goal is to use the money from the refinance to buy additional distressed properties, starting the process over again.

The key difference between BRRRR and traditional real estate investing is that it focuses on distressed properties. These properties are typically underpriced because they need significant repairs and renovations, offering investors an opportunity to purchase below market value. Once these properties are renovated, they can be rented out, allowing investors to refinance the property and pull out equity to fund future investments.

1. Buy the Property

The first step is purchasing a distressed property. Distressed properties are often sold for a lower price due to their condition, which makes them an attractive option for investors. However, it's important to carefully assess the property's condition and ensure that the cost of repairs will not exceed the potential value added by the renovations. Distressed properties typically require significant repairs, ranging from cosmetic improvements to more substantial structural work.

Before purchasing, investors should calculate the after-repair value (ARV) of the property. ARV is the estimated value of the property once the renovations are completed. By using comparable properties in the area, investors can estimate how much the property will be worth after repairs and decide if the potential return justifies the investment. You can consider using the 70 percent rule. This rule suggests that you should never pay more than 70 percent of the ARV minus the cost of repairs. For example, if a property's ARV is $300,000 and the estimated repair costs are $30,000, you should aim to pay no more than $189,000 for the property. This helps to ensure that you're purchasing the property at a price that allows room for profit after repairs (Nowacki 2024).

2. Rehab the Property

Once the property is acquired, the next step is to rehab or renovate the property. The goal here is to bring the property up to code, make necessary structural repairs, and improve its overall appeal to future tenants. Rehabbing can range from simple cosmetic upgrades, such as painting and flooring, to more complex structural repairs like replacing the roof or plumbing.

It's important to focus on improvements that will provide the highest return on investment. Key areas to target include kitchens, bathrooms, curb appeal, and energy-efficient upgrades. Before starting the rehab, create a realistic budget and timeline to ensure that the project stays on track. Overestimating the property's value or underestimating the cost of repairs can quickly turn a profitable venture into a costly one (Nowacki 2024).

3. Rent Out the Property

Once the property is repaired and move-in ready, it's time to find tenants. Renting the property allows you to generate steady income to cover the costs of the mortgage, insurance, taxes, and maintenance. This rental income will also help to build equity in the property over time.

Setting the right rent price is important, as we discussed earlier. It should be affordable for tenants while still covering your costs and generating a positive cash flow. Research comparable rental rates in the area to ensure your rent is competitive yet profitable. If the rent is set too high, you may struggle to attract tenants, and if it's too low, you might not generate enough cash flow to cover your expenses (Nowacki 2024).

4. Refinance the Property

Once the property is rented out and has begun to appreciate in value due to the renovations, you can refinance the mortgage. A cash-out refinance allows you to take out a larger mortgage than the original one, using the increased value of the property as collateral. The difference between the new mortgage and the existing mortgage is given to you in cash, which can be used to fund your next investment.

Not all cash-out refinance options are created equal. Compare different lenders to find the best rates and terms for your refinance. Be sure to factor in all costs, including closing costs and appraisals, when evaluating your options.

It's important to note that refinancing typically requires a minimum amount of time that you must own the property before applying for a cash-out refinance. Lenders may also require an appraisal to determine the property's new value and ensure that it meets their lending requirements. In addition, refinancing comes with closing costs, which should be factored into your financial plan (Nowacki 2024).

5. Repeat the Process

The final step in the BRRRR Method is to repeat the process with the cash from the refinance. The funds pulled out from the refinance can be used to purchase another distressed property to rehab, rent, and refinance. Over time, this creates a self-sustaining cycle that allows you to grow your portfolio without constantly needing to invest new capital.

The key to success with the BRRRR Method is effectively managing each stage of the process and maintaining a disciplined approach to reinvesting profits into new properties. While the BRRRR Method offers significant potential rewards, it also comes with its risks. Here are some of the main advantages and disadvantages to consider:

Pros:

- **Passive Income**: The rental properties generate consistent cash flow that can be used to cover your mortgage and other expenses, providing a passive income stream.
- **Building Equity**: Over time, your properties will increase in value, allowing you to build equity that can be used to purchase more properties.
- **Diversification**: The BRRRR Method allows you to

diversify your investment portfolio by acquiring multiple properties in different locations or markets.

Cons:

- **Costly and Time-Consuming Rehab**: Renovating properties can be expensive and time-consuming. Poor budgeting or unexpected issues can eat into your profits.
- **Risk of Loans**: Hard money loans and other short-term financing options often come with higher interest rates and fees, which can increase your overall investment costs.
- **Unforeseen Issues**: Properties may have hidden problems that could lead to higher-than-expected repair costs or difficulty attracting tenants (Nowacki 2024).

One example of someone who has had great success with BRRRR is Sean Sloop. In 2020, Sean teamed up with a colleague to scale his real estate portfolio more rapidly, focusing on cash flow as the ultimate goal. They decided to continue investing in the Lansing, MI market, where they had already seen success. Between August and December of 2020, they closed on four properties: three single-family homes and a duplex. Despite the challenges of the year, Sean remained committed to growing his portfolio, and each deal brought valuable lessons and results.

Property 1: A 3-bedroom, 1-bath home, purchased for $48,000 in August 2020. The rehab cost came in higher than expected, at $22,000, but the after-repair value (ARV) was much higher than anticipated, reaching $115,000, a far cry from the original estimate of $75,000.

Property 2: A 3-bedroom, 1-bath home purchased in October 2020 for $46,231. The rehab costs went over budget at $18,000, but the final ARV came in at $95,000, significantly higher than the estimated $70,000.

Property 3: A 4-bedroom, 1-bath home purchased for $37,500 in December 2020, part of a package deal with Property 4. Though the property was already tenanted and hadn't been updated yet, it provided steady cash flow. The ARV was estimated at $80,000.

Property 4: A 3-bedroom, 2-bath duplex, purchased in a package with Property 3 for $37,500. The rehab budget was set at $37,000, but after spending $40,000, the final ARV remained undetermined. This property was still in rehab at the time of refinancing.

In April 2021, after refinancing the three single-family homes, Sean was surprised by the appraisals, which came in far higher than expected. The market had risen, and favorable comps had popped up nearby, allowing them to refinance at significantly better terms than anticipated. The refinancing allowed them to pay off their line of credit, recover the rehab costs, and even put $30,000 in the bank for future deals.

However, not everything went smoothly. Sean learned several key lessons during this process. First, commercial financing proved to be more difficult than expected, with unfavorable terms like a short 15-year amortization and high interest rates. Despite calling over 20 banks, they were unable to secure the 25-year term they had hoped for. Second, Sean found out that DIY projects weren't as feasible as he had initially thought. Living an hour away from the properties, juggling a demanding day job, and not having the skill set to handle rehab work led to delays and budget overruns. He quickly realized that relying on contractors would have been more efficient in the long run.

Despite these setbacks, Sean and his partner are on track to scale further. With five units now in their portfolio, they plan to continue using the BRRRR strategy and expand into turnkey multifamily or portfolio properties. Their goal is to refine their financing options over time and eventually pay down parts of their portfolio to increase cash flow (Bigger Pockets 2021).

Reinvesting Profits for Long-Term Growth

Real estate investors are often drawn to rental properties for their capacity to generate substantial cash flow. This passive income offers more than just a means to cover monthly expenses—it opens doors to future growth and wealth-building opportunities. Many investors choose to reinvest rental property cash flow, maximizing returns and creating additional income streams. The decision to reinvest rental property cash flow depends on your long-term financial objectives. If you are satisfied with your current income, reinvesting may not seem necessary. However, if your goal is to grow your wealth or achieve financial independence, reinvesting your rental income could be an important strategy (Freeze 2024).

Choosing to reinvest rental profits creates opportunities for new income streams. Whether you acquire additional properties or invest in REITs, each reinvestment can contribute to your overall wealth. Over time, this compounding effect builds a diversified income base that supports long-term financial goals. Reinvesting cash flow can also accelerate your portfolio growth. By saving profits from one property, you can more quickly fund down payments for additional investments. This "snowball effect" allows investors to scale their portfolios, creating a cycle of increasing revenue and property acquisition. Finally, using rental cash flow to save for larger down payments on future properties can lead to improved financing options. A significant down payment reduces the size of your mortgage, potentially lowering your interest rate and eliminating private mortgage insurance. Larger down payments can also signal lower risk to lenders, resulting in more favorable loan terms (Freeze 2024).

Here are three ways to reinvest profits for long-term growth:

Purchase Another Investment Property

If you aim to build a portfolio of income-generating properties, using cash flow from one property to finance another is a logical step. Surplus profits from your current investments can be reinvested into acquiring additional real estate assets.

Real estate offers flexibility in investment strategies. For instance, you might purchase a property to renovate and sell for a profit or acquire another rental property to double your passive income. Expanding your portfolio through reinvestment boosts cash flow and provides the foundation for long-term financial success (Freeze 2024).

Invest in Real Estate Investment Trusts (REITs)

For those who prefer not to manage another physical property, REITS provides an alternative avenue to grow wealth. REITs allow investors to gain exposure to the real estate market without the responsibilities of property ownership.

By purchasing shares in companies that manage income-producing real estate, investors can generate returns similar to stocks. High-quality REITs often offer average annual returns between 8 percent and 10 percent, making them a viable option for passive income. This approach suits investors who wish to diversify their portfolios while avoiding the complexities of property management (Freeze 2024).

Remodel an Existing Property

Investing in upgrades for your current rental property is another way to reinvest cash flow and increase its value. Improvements can attract higher-quality tenants and justify increased rental rates, thereby enhancing your monthly income. Renovations such as updated kitchens, modern bathrooms, or energy-efficient features can also boost the property's resale value. When you eventually decide to sell, the return on your initial investment may be significantly higher. This strategy strengthens your real estate portfolio while improving the profitability of your existing assets (Freeze 2024).

Managing Multiple Properties: Tips for Efficiency

Managing multiple properties can feel like juggling several balls, each demanding your attention and precision. As your real estate portfolio grows, so does the complexity of keeping everything running smoothly.

One of the most pressing challenges is the increased time and effort required to oversee numerous properties. Each property demands unique care, from routine maintenance to tenant relations. Coordinating maintenance and repairs across several locations can become a logistical nightmare if not handled efficiently. You must keep a keen eye on all properties to check no issues are left unattended, as even minor problems can escalate into costly repairs it ignored. Additionally, keeping track of tenant communications and payments becomes increasingly complex. With multiple tenants, ensuring timely rent collection, addressing concerns, and maintaining open lines of communication requires a well-organized system to prevent anything from slipping through the cracks.

To tackle these challenges, implementing efficient property management strategies is crucial. One powerful tool that I recommend is property management software, which can streamline operations by automating tasks such as rent collection, maintenance scheduling, and tenant communication. Programs like Buildium or Rentec Direct offer features that help you manage properties remotely, providing real-time updates and alerts to keep you informed. Such software not only saves time but also reduces errors, ensuring you stay on top of every aspect of property management. If you prefer a more hands-on approach, hiring professional property management services may be a wise choice. A dedicated team can handle day-to-day operations, allowing you to focus on strategic growth. They can manage everything from tenant screening to maintenance coordination, providing peace of mind and freeing up your time to pursue new investment opportunities.

Creating standardized processes and checklists is another effective strategy to ensure consistency and efficiency across all properties. You can develop a set of procedures for common tasks such as tenant onboarding, maintenance requests, and rent collection. These processes should be clear and easy to follow, reducing the risk of mistakes and ensuring all team members are on the same page. Furthermore, you should prioritize tasks effectively to manage your properties efficiently. Identify high-priority tasks and urgent issues that require immediate attention, such as emergency repairs or tenant disputes. These should be dealt with as soon as possible to prevent escalation and minimize impact on both tenants and properties. Routine tasks, like regular maintenance checks or administrative duties, can be delegated to property managers or assistants.

Exit Strategies: Knowing When and How to Sell

Generally, the optimal strategy for holding real estate is never selling them. Retaining rental properties allows owners to benefit from ongoing inflation, which increases both rents and property values over time. Since the pandemic, inflation has surged, peaking at 9 percent in mid-2022 before leveling at approximately 3.3 percent (New Western 2024). By holding onto properties, you capitalize on this trend while avoiding the substantial costs associated with selling, such as commissions and long-term capital gains taxes.

While long-term ownership has advantages, there are times when selling an investment property aligns better with your needs and financial goals. Here are several scenarios when selling an investment property might be appropriate:

- A significant life event, such as a new family member, a death, a serious accident, a layoff, or a relocation, can create circumstances where selling an investment property is necessary to simplify life or access additional funds.
- If you have established greater sources of passive income, such as dividends, bond yields, or online income, and these sources require less active management than rental

properties, selling the property might become a more appealing option.

- When your property's capitalization rate (net rental yield) falls below the risk-free rate of return offered by investments like Treasury bonds, it may no longer provide adequate compensation for the risks and effort involved in managing it.

- Selling an investment property might make sense when you want to practice "Buy Utility, Rent Luxury" (BURL), using profits from high-cash-flow properties in less expensive areas to afford luxurious rental properties in premium locations.

- If the enjoyment or satisfaction you gain from owning the property diminishes and is outweighed by other priorities or investments that provide greater returns or fulfillment, selling may be a reasonable choice.

- When there is an expected increase in the local housing supply, such as a surge of new condos or developments, it might be wise to sell before oversupply drives property values down.

- If property taxes or other government-imposed costs become excessively burdensome and are projected to rise further, selling and relocating to a more tax-friendly jurisdiction or reinvesting in another area may be beneficial.

- If real estate accounts for more than 50 percent of your total net worth, diversifying into other asset classes by selling some of your properties can reduce financial risk and provide greater stability (New Western 2024).

Understanding Taxes When Selling a Property

When selling a rental property, understanding taxes is essential to protect your profits. One consideration is capital gains tax, which depends on how long you've owned the property, your income, and your filing status. If you sell a property you've owned for less than 12 months, you will incur short-term capital gains tax. This tax treats the profit as regular income, and you'll be taxed according to your income bracket. For instance, single filers earning up to $10,275 fall into the 10 percent tax bracket, while those earning over $539,900 are taxed at 37 percent. If you've owned the property for more than 12 months, long-term capital gains tax applies, which has lower rates: 0 percent, 15 percent, or 20 percent, based on your income. High-income earners also face an additional 3.8 percent net investment income surtax (New Western 2024).

Another tax to consider is the depreciation recapture tax. While you can claim property depreciation as a yearly expense, reducing your taxable rental income, the IRS requires you to pay back these deductions when you sell the property. Depreciation recapture is taxed as ordinary income, regardless of how long you've owned the property. For example, if you claimed $5,000 in depreciation annually for five years, you would owe tax on $25,000 upon selling. Even if you never claimed depreciation, the IRS still calculates recapture based on allowable deductions, making this tax unavoidable (New Western 2024).

To minimize tax liabilities, you can explore strategies like tax-loss harvesting, which offsets capital gains with investment losses. For example, selling underperforming stocks can balance gains from a rental property sale, reducing or even eliminating your capital gains tax. However, IRS rules, such as wash-sale restrictions, prevent reinvesting in substantially identical assets within 30 days of the sale. This strategy must be declared on IRS forms 8949 and 1040 (New Western 2024).

Another option is a 1031 exchange, which allows you to defer paying capital gains taxes by reinvesting proceeds into a similar property within strict timeframes. You have 45 days to identify a new property and 180 days to close the purchase. If deadlines aren't met, you'll owe the full tax amount. This strategy is ideal for those planning to continue real estate investing.

The Section 121 exclusion offers relief for investors converting a rental property into a primary residence. Single filers can exclude up to $250,000 of gains, while married filers can exclude $500,000. To qualify, you must own the property and live in it as your primary residence for at least two of the last five years. However, consulting a tax advisor is wise, as factors like depreciation recapture and previous exclusions can affect your tax savings (New Western 2024).

Lastly, you can consider using a self-directed IRA (SDIRA) to purchase real estate. While this method allows tax-advantaged investments, strict rules apply. You can't personally use the property or rent it to family members, and all expenses must be paid using IRA funds. A qualified SDIRA custodian can guide you through these requirements (New Western 2024).

In this chapter, we covered effective strategies for growing a real estate portfolio, starting with the BRRRR method and reinvesting profits. We also addressed the challenges of managing multiple properties and the advantages of adopting efficient systems or professional management services. Finally, we discussed factors to consider when deciding to sell a property. With these techniques, you can build a scalable, sustainable investment strategy that supports your financial goals and adapts to the evolving real estate market.

CHAPTER 9
PUTTING IT ALL TOGETHER

> *"Don't let obstacles stop you. Where there are obstacles, there is great opportunity."*

— DOTTIE HERMAN

You're standing at the summit of a mountain. The journey has been challenging, with steep climbs and unforeseen obstacles. Yet, the view from the top offers clarity, revealing the path you've traveled and the path ahead. This is where you stand now in your real estate investment journey. You've gathered knowledge, tools, and insights, preparing you to take your first confident steps into the world of property investment.

Now, we can put everything you've learned together. Here's a step-by-step guide to becoming a real estate investor:

1. **Develop your mindset**. The foundation of real estate investing begins with the right mindset. Embrace a long-term perspective, be open to learning continuously, and

build resilience against setbacks. Developing investor confidence comes through research, attending networking events, and learning from both the successes and failures of others in the industry.

2. **Set your financial goals**. Before making any investments, outline your financial objectives. Define your long-term vision—whether it's retiring early or building generational wealth—and break it down into medium-term goals (such as acquiring your first property) and short-term actions (like securing financing and finding suitable properties). This plan will guide your investment decisions.

3. **Locate potential properties**. Identify suitable properties by exploring various sources: real estate agents, the MLS, online auctions, or off-market opportunities like pre-foreclosures or foreclosures. Diversifying where you look increases your chances of finding profitable deals that align with your goals.

4. **Evaluate properties**. Carefully assess a property's value by reviewing its price history, comparing it to similar properties in the area, and seeking third-party appraisals when necessary. Understanding the market conditions and the specific value of a property guarantees that you're making an informed investment decision that will likely provide a good return.

5. **Inspect the condition of the house**. Conduct a thorough inspection to uncover potential issues such as structural damage, outdated systems, or costly repairs. This step makes sure you're not caught off guard by hidden costs and helps you make a decision about whether to proceed with the purchase, renegotiate the price, or walk away.

6. **Finance your investment.** Explore different financing options based on your financial situation. Traditional loans, hard money loans, and private money loans are common choices. Government-backed loans and creative financing strategies like seller financing or house hacking can also provide alternatives for those looking to enter the market with limited capital.

7. **Make the deal.** When you find the right property, prepare a competitive offer. This involves having your financing ready, determining the right offer price, and setting clear contingencies to protect yourself. Master negotiation techniques to secure a favorable deal and ensure you understand the closing process, including title searches, inspection reports, and final paperwork.

8. **Manage your properties.** Once you own a property, effective management is key to maintaining its value and profitability. Handle repairs promptly, maintain the property's curb appeal, and communicate openly with tenants. A good property management strategy reduces turnover and makes sure your property remains a steady source of income.

9. **Maximize cash flow.** Optimize rental income by setting competitive but fair rental prices based on the market. Reduce vacancy rates by keeping tenants happy with timely responses and quality living conditions. Managing expenses, such as property maintenance and utilities, helps preserve cash flow while leveraging tax deductions to ensure you keep more of your earnings.

10. **Manage risks.** Every investment carries some level of risk, but there are steps you can take to mitigate it. Protect your investments with appropriate insurance, such as landlord or property insurance, and consider

forming an LLC to shield your personal assets. Diversify your portfolio to reduce dependence on one property or market and create a contingency fund to cover unexpected expenses.

11. **Scale your portfolio.** To grow your real estate business, consider using strategies like BRRRR, which allows you to reinvest the same capital in multiple properties. Managing multiple properties efficiently can lead to greater passive income. Also, explore exit strategies, such as selling for a profit or rolling your investments into higher-value properties, to scale over time.

12. **Never worry about money again**. The goal of real estate investing is to build wealth that generates consistent, passive income streams. As you scale your portfolio, you'll create a financial cushion that can support you long-term. With careful planning, strategic reinvestment, and a growing number of income-generating properties, you can achieve financial freedom and the peace of mind that comes with never having to worry about money again.

Staying Updated: News, Blogs, and Podcasts

Before we say goodbye, I want to talk about the importance of staying updated. In the fast-paced world of real estate investing, staying informed is a necessity. Imagine the edge you gain by knowing market trends before they become common knowledge. This foresight allows you to identify emerging opportunities, adapt to market changes, and refine your strategies continually. Keeping abreast of industry news and trends ensures you're not left behind as regulations evolve, or new investment avenues open up. You can maintain a competitive edge and ensure your strategies are as effective as possible in a constantly shifting landscape.

Reliable news outlets like CNBC Real Estate and Bloomberg Real Estate provide timely updates on market conditions, economic forecasts, and regulatory changes. These platforms offer insights that can impact your investment decisions and provide a broader understanding of the economic forces at play. Meanwhile, blogs such as the BiggerPockets Blog and The Real Estate Guys delve into specific strategies and case studies, offering a more detailed look at real estate investing from seasoned professionals. These blogs cover a wide range of topics, from financing options to property management tips, making them invaluable resources for both new and experienced investors.

Podcasts offer another layer of insight, allowing you to learn while on the go. The Real Estate Investing Podcast and Apartment Building Investing with Michael Blank offer interviews, success stories, and expert advice, all of which can inform and inspire your own investing journey. These podcasts provide diverse perspectives, often featuring guests who have navigated unique challenges and achieved remarkable success. Listening to these stories can not only inform your strategy but also motivate you to persist through challenges and seek new opportunities.

Consuming content from diverse sources brings several benefits. It exposes you to different perspectives, broadening your understanding of the industry and sparking new ideas. Engaging with a mix of formats—be it articles, blogs, or podcasts—keeps information fresh and engaging, preventing learning fatigue. Additionally, learning from experienced professionals and experts through these mediums provides practical insights that can be directly applied to your investment activities. It's about building a well-rounded knowledge base that allows you to make informed decisions with confidence.

To effectively incorporate these sources into your daily routine, you can consider setting aside specific times each day or week for reading and listening. This could be during your morning commute, lunch break, or a designated "learning hour" in your schedule.

Let me end off with another success story that will show you just how important continuous learning is. Jeremy Iannuzzelli's journey to building a $2.5 million property portfolio on a $50,000 income wasn't an overnight success but rather a process rooted in diligent research, strategic decisions, and calculated risks.

At 22, Jeremy embarked on his property investment journey. He wasn't one to dive in without preparation. Instead, he spent a full year learning everything he could about the property market, attending at least five open houses every weekend, and observing auctions, guaranteeing he had a comprehensive understanding of the market before making his first move.

"I wasn't rushing," Jeremy recalls. "I wanted to get everything right, particularly the first property. You only get one shot at it, and it's too important to make mistakes early on."

That commitment paid off. After months of research, he was presented with an opportunity from an agent he'd developed a relationship with. A property that ticked all the boxes: a solid rental yield, close to key amenities and transport, and in a location with strong potential. With his pre-approved finance and a quick analysis of the numbers, Jeremy decided to move fast.

"I made a decision by 7:30 AM the next morning. It wasn't impulsive, but it was quick because I knew my research had given me the confidence to act."

This first property became the foundation of his portfolio. The rental yield was nearly 7 percent, meaning that the rent covered the mortgage and some of the costs, minimizing his exposure to debt. This focus on cash flow, he notes, is a crucial part of his strategy: "You have to make sure your investments can sustain themselves. It's about long-term gains, but having the cash flow to support the journey is what lets you sleep at night."

But even Jeremy's rapid success wasn't without roadblocks. After reaching his fourth property, the banks stopped lending to him. His borrowing capacity had reached its limit. However, by refinancing with a different lender, Jeremy was able to continue expanding his portfolio. "Sometimes, the traditional route isn't going to work, but there are always ways around it."

One of his key principles is maintaining a low loan-to-value ratio (currently 65 percent), which provides flexibility in case of unforeseen events. He also keeps a buffer of three months' worth of expenses for each property, ensuring peace of mind even during times when rental income might be delayed.

Jeremy's approach is simple but effective: focus on high cash-flow properties near major cities, where yields are strong and growth is inevitable over time. And while others might follow trends, Jeremy prefers to get in early, buying when the market is still under the radar. He's done this successfully in places like Queensland, Australia, where he invested ahead of the crowd, securing high-yield properties before they became competitive.

By the time Jeremy reached his fifth property, he had built a portfolio that was generating enough income to support itself. But it wasn't just his investments that set him up for success. Living at home with his parents for the first few years saved him significant amounts on living expenses, allowing him to reinvest his savings into more properties. While not everyone has that option, Jeremy believes that anyone can build a successful portfolio with determination and smart financial management.

Looking back on his journey, Jeremy has no regrets. His strategic approach, commitment to research, and ability to overcome challenges allowed him to build a portfolio worth $2.5 million. His story serves as a reminder that success in property investing isn't about taking massive risks but about making calculated decisions, managing risks effectively, and taking the right actions at the right time (Sweeney 2015).

In this chapter, we covered the essential steps to becoming a successful real estate investor. From developing the right mindset and setting clear financial goals to managing properties and scaling your portfolio, each step builds a foundation for your long-term success. With the knowledge of property evaluation, financing options, and risk management, you're equipped to navigate the challenges of real estate investing. Furthermore, staying updated through reliable news outlets, blogs, and podcasts will keep you informed and help you adapt to an ever-changing market. As you take your first steps into real estate, remember that persistence, learning, and strategy are key to securing financial freedom and creating wealth that lasts. Now, let's hear some inspirational stories from some experts to help you take your first step in real estate investing.

CHAPTER 10

EXPERT VOICES: REAL STORIES, REAL ADVICE, REAL SUCCESS

R eal estate is an experience, not just a transaction. You must learn from every step, grow with every challenge, and, most importantly, listen to those who have walked the path before you. While the previous chapters have given you the tools and knowledge to start your real estate ventures, this chapter offers something just as valuable: real-world insights from seasoned professionals.

Each expert featured in this chapter brings a unique perspective shaped by years of experience in real estate. They've gone through the highs and lows, mastered the art of negotiation, and discovered strategies that turn investments into sources of long-term wealth. Their stories will inspire you, and their tips will provide actionable guidance as you begin investing in real estate.

Experience is the best teacher, but it doesn't always have to be your own. Learning from others' experiences allows you to avoid costly mistakes, capitalize on proven strategies, and gain the confidence to take bold steps. The professionals featured here have a collective wealth of knowledge that will help you fast-track your success in real estate.

Each expert will guide you through their personal story, sharing significant moments that shaped their career. These stories are lessons on resilience, adaptability, and creativity. You'll see how they approached challenges, overcame obstacles, and stayed committed to their goals.

Following their stories, each individual will provide three actionable tips focused on the most critical aspects of real estate investing. Whether it's advice on finding the right property, securing financing, or managing risk, these tips are distilled from years of hard-earned experience.

As you read through this chapter, keep a notebook handy. Jot down the tips and strategies that stick out to you and consider how they align with your goals. Reflect on the stories and consider how you can apply their lessons to your investing strategy.

Use this chapter for inspiration and as a valuable resource. Let these experts remind you that success in real estate is attainable, regardless of your starting point. They were once beginners as well, and now they are here to guide you.

Allow their stories and tips to be the motivation you need to take action. This is just the beginning; with the knowledge from this book and the insights from the experts in this chapter, you have everything you need to succeed.

Randy Utz, Owner | Associate Broker | Investor with VR Group of EXP Realty

My real estate investing experience began behind a computer screen in a 6'x6' felt-lined cubicle filled with dust and desperation for something more. After countless hours of searching for a new career path, one with purpose and a much bigger upside, real estate always seemed to resonate most.

In 2014, I decided to get my real estate license and dive into real estate sales, all while maintaining my W-2 desk job. I loved everything about selling real estate; it was fast-paced, thrilling, and very rewarding both personally and monetarily. Fast-forward to 2018, I had some experience under my belt and a decent book of business for only selling real estate on nights and weekends. My second son had just been born earlier that summer, and I was fed up with my 9 to 5. I put in my letter of resignation, scared out of my mind. It was time to sink or swim.

Shortly after I became a full-time real estate sales professional, I received a phone call from a real estate investor named James looking for an agent with 'experience in flipping houses.' By that point in my career, I had only helped clients buy and sell their personal homes. However, I had watched hours of BiggerPockets videos, listened to dozens of podcasts, and did not miss an episode of Flip or Flop, so obviously, I was the perfect guy for the job. All jokes aside, I had no clue, but it was a calculated risk because I was willing to figure it out. Through helping James, I gained real-life knowledge, experience, connections, and confidence to invest for myself.

Today, I have invested and participated in a wide variety of real estate investments, including Wholesales, Flips, Long-Term Rentals, Short-Term Rentals, and Commercial (including Multi-family, Office, Retail, and Industrial). In addition, I am still very active in real estate sales both personally and through my real estate team. The experience and knowledge from both the investing and sales side of real estate have exponentially accelerated my career in both.

Randy's Tips for New Investors

My first tip for new investors is that there is never a perfect time to invest, and you will never feel 100% ready. Let me be clear: I am not saying to start investing without educating yourself. However, there are only so many videos, podcasts, and social media gurus you can listen to before taking action. If I had waited until I felt ready or knew everything, I would still be rotting away in that cubicle. I was terrified when I left the security of my W-2 job for real estate sales with a two-year-old and a newborn at home, but I did. In no way did I feel confident enough to advise an experienced investor in the early part of my sales career, but I did. Learn the fundamentals and figure the rest out on the ride.

My next tip is to find a Mentor. Look for someone who is doing what you aspire to do. What is even better is someone local to you so that you can physically visit their properties and shadow them.

Most successful investors are open books if you approach them with a willingness to listen and act on their advice.

Finally, don't chase shiny objects. In real estate investing, there is no shortage of options. This can leave you jumping from Flips to Rentals to Syndications and everything in between without ever having actually done a deal. My advice for a new investor is to pick one type of investment for your first deal and see it through before trying anything else. You may love it or hate it, but either way, you will learn plenty of lessons that will translate into other types of real estate investing.

Sherri Verdon, Real Estate Agent for ReMax One

When I got married to my husband, a dedicated DC police officer, I moved from New Jersey to Maryland to begin our life together. Maryland was unfamiliar, and being far from my family and roots was difficult. But with this change came opportunities I could never have foreseen. By sheer luck and timing, I interviewed and was hired for a position as an assistant to a sales representative for a major homebuilder in the area. I knew I wasn't the most experienced candidate, but I worked tirelessly to prove that I was willing to learn and ready for the challenge.

Not long after, I was promoted to a sales manager role overseeing a remote community. The community wasn't selling previously, and I had my work cut out for me. I poured my heart and energy into the job, determined to turn things around. Within two months, I sold 10 homes. It was a turning point, and the builder took notice. They promoted me to manage their flagship community in Calvert County, a position that would change the course of my career and my life.

For eight years, I worked in Calvert County, first building out a 22-home community and then managing and building an adjacent neighborhood of 88 homes. I found immense fulfillment in helping families bring their dreams to life. But what truly enriched my experience were the relationships I built along the way. I made it a point to understand my clients—their stories, their aspirations, and what they envisioned for their futures.

I eventually built my own home in the community I managed, surrounded by the people I had helped. My clients became friends and neighbors. This created a sense of family in Maryland that eased the distance from my New Jersey roots. Over a decade later, I still feel blessed to live in a place filled with love, connection, and the memories of the work I poured my heart into.

When the community neared completion, I decided to set off on a new adventure as an independent real estate agent. The transition from new construction to resale came with its own challenges, but I was determined. In my first year as an individual agent, I sold $10 million in real estate transactions—a testament to the relationships I had cultivated over the years. Referrals poured in from past clients who trusted me, and I continued to prioritize serving my clients with the same passion and care.

Today, I sell between $10 million and $20 million in real estate as an individual agent annually. This career has given me the freedom to create the life I dreamed of—balancing my work with time for my family, while also serving others through my profession. It's been a blessing to help people make one of the most significant decisions of their lives.

One of the most valuable lessons I've learned comes from my mother, who always said, "Everyone has a story and a struggle. Look for their story. Learn their story, and you'll know how to help them. In doing so, you will find and fulfill your own meaningful purpose on this Earth." Early in my career, I met a couple designing their new home. The husband was visibly anxious and had to step away several times during the contract process. When I gently inquired, I learned he was going blind and was struggling to read the documents. That moment changed a lot for me. I made it my mission to design a home that would help him live comfortably with his disability by incorporating thoughtful touches like well-placed lighting and an open layout.

That couple became more than just clients—they became my friends. The husband played Santa Claus at our neighborhood Christmas party for years, and his wife gifted me handmade ornaments that I cherish to this day. Stories like theirs remind me of why I do what I do and the incredible impact this career has allowed me to make.

Sherri's Tips for New Investors

If I could give advice to anyone starting in real estate, it would be this: lead with your heart. Invest in your clients emotionally, value every opportunity, and approach your work with humility and gratitude. Success will follow when you put others first. Every transaction is a chance to make a difference in someone's life. By staying true to that purpose, you'll find success, happiness, and fulfillment beyond what you ever thought possible.

Noah Dodson, President of Provision Property Management

When I first entered the world of real estate, I never thought I would manage so many properties across Maryland. I began my career as a leasing agent, mainly showing apartments and answering tenant questions. While it was a simple job, I became curious about how the entire property management process worked, the relationships I built with tenants, and the systems that made everything run smoothly.

One day, a landlord I worked with surprised me by offering me the chance to manage ten of his properties. "You have the organization and drive to do this," he said. Even though I wasn't sure I was prepared, I decided to take a chance and accepted the challenge.

The beginning was tough. I spent my first few months juggling maintenance requests, tenant issues, and late-night calls. I quickly learned that property management doesn't just involve fixing problems. It also requires being proactive and preventing issues before they arise.

One memorable challenge came during a storm that caused flooding at several properties. Tenants were worried, and landlords were anxious about the possible expenses. Instead of panicking, I worked with contractors and local officials to resolve the situation. What could have been a crisis strengthened my reputation for handling challenging situations.

Now, I manage various properties, from Baltimore's urban apartments to Calvert County's suburban homes. Each property has unique challenges, but what motivates me is making life easier for tenants and landlords. Success means building relationships and consistently offering value.

Noah's Tips for New Investors

My first piece of advice is to communicate clearly and often. Whether dealing with tenants or landlords, being transparent and open in communication is necessary. Listen to concerns, respond quickly, and set clear expectations.

My next tip is to establish systems from the start. Don't wait until you're overwhelmed to set up processes. Create systems for collecting rent, screening tenants, and tracking maintenance immediately. It will save you time and stress later on.

And finally, I recommend that you stay ahead of problems. Being proactive is key to long-term success. Regular property checks and routine maintenance help catch small issues before they turn into costly repairs.

Reflecting on my life spent working in real estate, I see how every experience—from leasing apartments to managing numerous properties—has taught me valuable lessons. Property management goes beyond fixing things and collecting rent. The real lesson is in building harmonious relationships between landlords and tenants.

For those just starting, my advice is straightforward: focus on clear communication, set up systems early on, and always be proactive. These habits will save you time and money while helping you build trust with everyone you work with. Property management can be challenging, but seeing the positive impact of your work on people's lives is incredibly rewarding.

Remember, no one becomes an expert overnight. Take each step as it comes, learn from your experiences, and don't hesitate to seek help when needed. Success comes from being consistent, adaptable, and eager to improve.

Good luck on your journey—you've got this!

Shad Montague, President of Clear Vision Property Management, President of Next Level Investment Funding, Montague Investments Team Lead with Montague Properties with eXp Realty

In looking back at the beginning, as a real estate investor, my goals were simple. I just wanted to flip houses. All I desired to do was buy an ugly, gross house and do all the right things to make it a great home for a family. My goal from the start was to do the best job possible and make something I was proud of. Although I had a real estate license, I knew little about real estate investing, because I thought only people with money were able to do that. And I did NOT start off quickly. I was stuck looking for the perfect deal...for almost two years! I started thinking that I had to make a move soon, or I would never jump into the real estate investing world.

Finally, I found a house to flip that was on my street! As I fought through several hurdles in the buying process, I saw that you must be knowledgeable and have a great team to be successful. Once I owned this shell of a house, I now had to hire everyone; framers, roofers, electricians, and plumbers, as well as learn what was required to install a septic tank and well. I learned quickly that not everyone had the same vision as I did. I was told numerous times that there was no way that I would be successful, and contractors wouldn't even entertain the idea of working with me. This was just reinforcement to me that this was a challenge and that I was going to be successful. I ended up finding some amazing team members. We put the house together and made my first flip a resounding success.

Since then, I have learned that there are so many ways to work as a real estate investor and I am still looking for more ways to grow. While I still flip houses, my biggest growth as an investor and in my net worth has been building a portfolio. I wish I knew then how much of an impact buy and hold properties have on your net worth growth over the long term. My one regret is that I didn't keep more houses.

That was 15 years ago and after hundreds of properties, I have learned that to be an entrepreneur, you can't have limiting beliefs. You must continue to learn and grow your toolbox so that you are able to see more opportunities. This is one of the biggest reasons I started an investment networking group in my area to teach about real estate investing. Standing in front of your peers and speaking about real estate requires you to always have an open mind. When I started, the goal was to flip houses. Now we own many segments of real estate, from residential, short-term rentals, multi units, commercial and even a property management company. On any given day, I will wear many hats. From contractor, Agent, investor, developer, property manager and landlord. I truly look at a property and form it into a vision that opens it up to its most profitable use.

Shad's Tips for New Investors

From my experience, there are three keys to success. My first piece of advice is to make your money going into the deal. This is my number one rule. Never believe that a property is going to appreciate in value as a hope. Always look at the numbers because they are our report card that doesn't lie. Don't ever be afraid to walk away from a deal if it is too hard, or you are battling to try to make it profitable. If it doesn't work, move on. There will be more opportunity. Think in abundance.

My next tip is to be diversified in real estate. So many people who want to get into real estate investing spend so much time listening to those that have no reason to be giving advice. I have found that the chicken littles that say the sky is falling in real estate don't understand that as one area of real estate is declining, another area is expanding.

And my final tip is don't be over leveraged. While the biggest impact on net worth in real estate is leveraged growth, you always need to remember that real estate runs in cycles. You need to be able to move in and out of opportunities as the market dictates. Don't get to a point where you have to sell at a discount.

Melanie Montague, CEO of Montague Properties, Team Lead with eXp Realty

Where do I begin with my story? Let's start after I spent several years as a Realtor in the Southern Maryland area. I was introduced to a local investor who was working under someone else who started a successful investor coaching program. This was during the REO/foreclosure boom around 2008 and 2009. In our area, we were seeing about 40-50 percent of all homes listed on the market categorized as a distressed home, either as a foreclosure or a short sale. This market was tough due to lack of ability for buyers to obtain financing. Because of these market conditions, I learned the art of maneuvering the short sale market and how to represent sellers to get them out of the home they could no longer afford.

I liked what this investor was doing, so I decided to work with him to grow his business. I thought that doing this would help me with sales because if I could land multiple investors, I was guaranteed 6-8 sales from each of them per year. After working closely with him through all his workshops, I thought that we can do this ourselves. It was not as hard as it once seemed to be, and I learned firsthand how to evaluate a potential property for profit. This includes the actual cost of the renovation, the "on no" did not see that coming buffer, and everything in between. My husband and I were then presented with the chance to take on a HUGE project that most would be afraid to tackle, and we agreed it was a great opportunity. We had several contractors look at the project, and only a few could see our vision. Most thought the property was a teardown. We renovated the home and sold it for a nice profit. And with that, our first major project was complete. That is how we got into the flipping side of investing. We had already owned a few rental properties, and we had dreams of owning more. I thought that the flipping side of real estate investing would help get us the funds to do just that. So, we put the two methods together to grow our long-term passive income side of investing in real estate. It was a great experience and truthfully set us on our path today! I'm very grateful for the opportunities that happened, and we were able to see what the outcome could be because it truthfully molded us to have open minds and visions of what this life could be if we just think outside of the box.

My experience as a Realtor and Investor has so much further to go! My husband and I are always

looking at what is happening in the market to see if the new opportunities presented are something we are interested in learning more about. When they do interest us, we seek people who have the knowledge in those areas and study the opportunity. Sometimes we need to get creative and step out of our comfort zone, but that is where you do most of your growing. We have created a fantastic network around us of very smart investors, so if we do not know an answer, someone we know can help us. Not only that, but we stay focused and always evaluate where we are and where we want to be. If we fail, then we view it as a great learning tool and will use it to be successful next time! The sky is the limit, and we continue to push forward and learn so we can build an empire that is strong and sustainable for the future. I always wanted to work for myself.... and it is my mindset and perseverance that has made it possible.

Melanie's Tips for New Investors

I have three main tips for beginners. My first is to get as much education and knowledge regarding real estate investing as you can. Pair up with someone, take a class, get a mentor, and ask a lot of questions. II also recommend that you don't let fear step in your way. Muster up your courage and make the move, or you never will. Lastly, never stop learning. There will always be new opportunities, and you will need to be open to learning to see them. Take the time to listen and learn daily, even if you think you've seen it all.

Success in real estate doesn't just involve about luck; it also involves persistence, knowledge, and the ability to take informed action. The stories and strategies shared in this chapter demonstrate that with the right mindset and guidance, anyone can achieve financial independence through real estate. Every expert you've read about started as a beginner who faced challenges and persevered to reach their goals. Their experiences remind us that no matter where you are with real estate investing, growth and success are attainable realities.

Now, it's your turn. Take what you've learned, apply the insights, and start making progress. Whether it's securing your first deal, expanding your portfolio, or refining your investment strategy, the key is to keep learning and moving forward. The path to success is built on action, and the knowledge you've gained from this book is your foundation. Real estate has the power to revolutionize your financial future. Believe in yourself, stay committed, and take the next step toward the wealth and freedom you deserve. Your next step is significant. Don't hesitate to take it now.

CONCLUSION

As we reach the end of this guide, it's time to reflect on the journey we've taken together through the world of real estate investing. We've navigated the essential steps, strategies, and insights that form the backbone of successful property investment. From building a resilient mindset to mastering property management, each chapter has equipped you with the tools needed to embark on a rewarding real estate venture.

In the beginning, we laid the groundwork by exploring the importance of a proactive mindset.

In Chapter 1, we laid the foundation for your real estate investment journey by exploring the core reasons to invest in real estate. We covered how real estate can provide tax benefits, build wealth, and create financial independence. The chapter emphasized the importance of cultivating the right mindset and investor confidence to tackle challenges and embrace opportunities. We discussed how adopting a growth-oriented perspective can transform challenges into opportunities. Just as I recovered from my personal struggles from my time serving overseas, you can recover from whatever circumstances you live with.

Chapter 2 focused on the steps of finding and evaluating properties. We discussed various methods to locate potential properties, such as using real estate agents, MLS listings, online auctions, and off-market opportunities like foreclosures. The chapter also covered how to assess property values through market analysis, appraisals, and third-party inspections to ensure you're making informed investment decisions.

In Chapter 3, we delved into the diverse financing options available for first-time investors. We delved into creative financing methods that open doors to real estate even when traditional pathways seem blocked. Techniques like house hacking and partnerships provide flexible options for those just starting out. We examined traditional loans, hard money loans, private money loans, and creative financing strategies like seller financing and crowdfunding. The chapter also addressed practical considerations like building credit and using home equity to fund investments.

Chapter 4 explored the process of making the deal, from building a strong network to creating competitive offers. We walked through the steps of submitting an offer, negotiating terms, and preparing for the closing process. Mastering negotiation tactics was also emphasized to help secure the best possible deal.

Chapter 5 provided a detailed guide to managing properties effectively. This chapter covered the essentials of property management, including handling maintenance and repairs, upgrading properties, and managing tenants. It also focused on financial management practices and understanding landlord-tenant laws to guarantee smooth operations.

In Chapter 6, we discussed strategies for maximizing cash flow. Topics included determining the right rental rate, reducing vacancy rates, managing expenses efficiently, and leveraging tax benefits to keep more of your earnings. The chapter provided actionable steps to optimize income and profitability.

Chapter 7 was dedicated to risk management. We discussed how to protect investments with the right insurance, including landlord insurance and forming an LLC to safeguard personal assets. The chapter also covered the importance of diversifying your portfolio and building a contingency fund to prepare for unexpected expenses.

Chapter 8 provided a roadmap for scaling your portfolio. We introduced the BRRRR strategy as a way to maximize growth. The chapter also explored reinvesting profits, managing multiple properties, and considering exit strategies when it's time to sell. Understanding taxes in the selling process was also discussed to help you make informed decisions as you grow your investment portfolio.

Chapter 9 brought everything together, providing a comprehensive review of the steps covered in the book and reinforcing how to integrate these strategies for long-term success. This chapter served as a culmination of the principles and techniques that will guide you in building a prosperous real estate investment career.

Finally, Chapter 10, showed us that real estate investing is a path of learning, persistence, and taking action. The insights shared in this chapter prove that success is achievable for anyone willing to commit, adapt, and apply the right strategies. Now, it's your turn to take the next step, embrace the opportunities ahead, and start building your path to financial freedom.

If you ever need additional support or resources, remember that you're not alone. I am here, along with a community of seasoned investors and professionals, ready to offer guidance and encouragement. The world of real estate is vast, and there are countless resources available to help you along the way.

As a former Marine with over two decades of experience in finance, my mission has always been to empower you with the knowledge and confidence to achieve prosperity. I am deeply committed to your success and I am here to support you at every stage of your journey. Remember to find that mentor that aligns with your ambitions. Put a mini agreement together where you are doing all the action, while they are there to guide you so that one day you will be that boss leading by example who everyone gravitates around!

Real estate investing holds the promise of financial freedom and long-term wealth. While challenges may arise, the rewards are worth the effort. Stay resilient, keep learning, and embrace each opportunity with enthusiasm. Remember, every successful investor started where you are now, but you have to take the first step! With determination and the right strategies, you can build a future filled with financial stability and fulfillment.

If you found this book helpful or empowering in your real estate journey, we'd love to hear from you! Your feedback not only helps us improve but also supports others looking to take their first step toward financial independence. Please consider leaving a review to share your experience.

As you move forward, may you find inspiration in each step, the discipline to keep failing forward, and the courage to thrive with your mindset within every challenge. The path to success is paved with actions, learning, and a growth mindset. Your journey begins now, and I am honored to be a part of it. Here's to your success and the exciting adventures that lie ahead in the world of real estate investing.

REFERENCES

Araj, Victoria. 2024. "What Is House Hacking and Is It Something You Should Be Doing?" Rocket Mortgage. April 3, 2024. https://www.rocketmortgage.com/learn/house-hacking

Azdari, Mason. 2023. "How to Thoroughly Inspect the Condition of a House." Owner Inspections. October 3, 2023. https://ownerinspections.com.au/inspecting-house-condition-guide/.

Bankwest. n.d. "Why Invest in Property?" Accessed 19 December 2024. https://www.bankwest.com.au/personal/home-buying/guides/benefits-of-property-investment

20 Famous Real Estate Investing Quotes https://www.realtymogul.com/knowledge-center/article/20-famous-real-estate-investing-quotes

Bigger Pockets. 2021. "2020 BRRRR Success Story – Lessons Learned." https://www.biggerpockets.com/forums/311/topics/950584-2020-brrrr-success-story-lessons-learned

Bigger Pockets. 2024. "My House Hack Success Story." https://www.biggerpockets.com/forums/88/topics/1222271-my-house-hack-success-story

Consumer Financial Protection Bureau. 2024. "How do I get and keep a good credit score?" December 12, 2024. https://www.consumerfinance.gov/ask-cfpb/how-do-i-get-and-keep-a-good-credit-score-en-318/

Downey, Lucas. 2024. "Closing: What It Is, How It Works, Requirements." Investopedia. October 28, 2024. https://www.investopedia.com/terms/c/closing.asp.

Freeze, Patrick. 2024. "3 Common Ways to Reinvest Rental Property Cash Flow." Bay Property Management Group. August 13, 2024. https://www.baymgmtgroup.com/blog/reinvest-rental-property-cash-flow/

Gariepy, Laura. 2024. "Top 6 Tax Benefits of Real Estate Investing." Rocket Mortgage. April 24, 2024. https://www.rocketmortgage.com/learn/tax-benefits-of-real-estate-investing

Goodreads. 2024. "A Quote by Franklin D. Roosevelt." https://www.goodreads.com/quotes/10334663-real-estate-cannot-be-lost-or-stolen-nor-can-it.

Hill, Jerald Lee. 2024. "Crowdfunding in real estate: opportunities and risks." Jerald Lee Hill. November 21, 2024. https://jeraldleehill.com/crowdfunding-in-real-estate-opportunities-and-risks/

Lake, Rebecca. 2024. "The Complete Guide to Financing an Investment Property." Investopedia. June 17, 2024. https://www.investopedia.com/articles/investing/021016/complete-guide-financing-investment-property.asp.

Luxon, Ben. 2023. "The Landlord's Complete Guide To Rental Property Management." Landlord Studio. December 29, 2023. https://www.landlordstudio.com/blog/rental-property-management-guide

Macquarie Bank. n.d. "6 Property Negotiation Tips You Need To Know." Accessed 20 December, 2024. https://www.macquarie.com.au/home-loans/property-negotiation-tips.html

McCall, Melissa. 2024. "Landlord-Tenant Law." Find Law. November 4, 2024. https://www.findlaw.com/realestate/landlord-tenant-law.html

Money Smart. 2024. "Save for an Emergency Fund." https://moneysmart.gov.au/saving/save-for-an-emergency-fund.

Moore, Paul. 2021. "How to Do a Real Estate Market Analysis." Bigger Pockets. June 25, 2021. https://www.biggerpockets.com/guides/real-estate-market-analysis?utm_source=chatgpt.com.

MRI. 2024. "An Oasis of Innovation – the Rent Manager User Conference." MRI Software. June 11, 2024. https://www.mrisoftware.com/blog/building-diversified-real-estate-investment-portfolio-minimize-risk/.

New Western. 2024. "Step by Step Guide on Selling Your Investment Property Like the Pros." https://www.newwestern.com/guide/selling-a-rental-property/

Nowacki, Lauren. 2024. "Understanding the BRRRR Method of Real Estate Investment." Rocket Mortgage. May 16, 2024. https://www.rocketmortgage.com/learn/brrrr

Property Chat. 2023. "Success with off-market deals?" March 22, 2023. https://www.propertychat.com.au/community/threads/success-with-off-market-deals-atypical-strategies.71358/

Reed, Eric. 2021. "How to Set Smart Goals for Your Investments." Smart Asset. August 19, 2021. https://smartasset.com/investing/investment-goals

Rent Better. 2024. "Tips for Calculating Rental Price." https://rentbetter.com.au/article/tips-for-calculating-the-rental-price

Rohde, Jeff. 2024. "How to Protect Your Real Estate Assets: 6 Strategies to Know." Www.stessa.com. https://www.stessa.com/blog/how-to-protect-real-estate-assets/.

Steinberg, Steven. 2024. "How to Find Investment Properties: A Guide." Rocket Mortgage. https://www.rocketmortgage.com/learn/how-to-find-investment-properties.

Stevens, Richard. 2024. "3 Highly Motivational Real Estate Success Stories." New Silver. January 25, 2024. https://newsilver.com/the-lender/real-estate-success-stories/.

Sutton, Spencer. 2024. "3 Ways to Decrease Vacancy Rates for Your Rental Property." Evernest. February 15, 2024. https://www.evernest.co/blog/3-ways-to-decrease-vacancy-rates-for-your-rental-property.

Sweeney, Nila. 2015. "How I built my $2.5m portfolio on a $50k income." Your Investment Property." November 5, 2015. https://www.yourinvestmentpropertymag.com.au/success-stories/how-i-built-my-2-5m-portfolio-on-a-50k-income

Wall Street Prep. n.d. "Property Value." Accessed 19 December, 2024. https://www.wallstreetprep.com/knowledge/property-value/

Wood, Kate. 2024. "How to Make an Offer on a House." Nerd Wallet. August 17, 2024. https://www.nerdwallet.com/article/mortgages/making-an-offer-on-a-house.

www.ingramcontent.com/pod-product-compliance
Lightning Source LLC
Chambersburg PA
CBHW061800120626
46550CB00005B/2075